ATLA BIBLIOGRAPHY SERIES
edited by Dr. Kenneth E. Rowe

1. *A Guide to the Study of the Holiness Movement,* by Charles Edwin Jones. 1974.
2. *Thomas Merton: A Bibliography,* by Marquita E. Breit. 1974.
3. *The Sermon on the Mount: A History of Interpretation and Bibliography,* by Warren S. Kissinger. 1975.
4. *The Parables of Jesus: A History of Interpretation and Bibliography,* by Warren S. Kissinger, 1975.
5. *Homosexuality and the Judeo-Christian: An Annotated Bibliography,* by Thom Horner. 1981.
6. *A Guide to the Study of the Pentacostal Movement,* by Charles Edwin Jones. 1983.
7. *The Genesis of Modern Process Thought: A Historical Outline with Bibliography,* by George R. Lucas, Jr. 1983.
8. *A Presbyterian Bibliography,* by Harold B. Prince. 1983.
9. *Paul Tillich: A Comprehensive Bibliography,* by Richard C. Crossman. 1983.
10. *A Bibliography of the Samaritans,* by Alan David Crown. 1984. (see no. 32).
11. *An Annotated and Classified Bibliography of English Literature Pertaining to the Ethiopian Orthodox Church,* by Jon Bonk. 1984.
12. *International Meditation Bibliography, 1950 to 1982,* by Howard R. Jarrell. 1984.
13. *Rabindranath Tagore: A Bibliography,* by Katherine Henn. 1985.
14. *Research in Ritual Studies: A Programmatic Essay and Bibliography,* by Ronald L. Grimes. 1985.
15. *Protestant Theological Education in America,* by Heather F. Day. 1985.
16. *Unconscious: A Guide to Sources,* by Natalino Caputi. 1985.
17. *The New Testament Apocrypha and Pseudepigrapha,* by James H. Charlesworth. 1987.
18. *Black Holiness,* by Charles Edwin Jones. 1987.
19. *A Bibliography on Ancient Ephesus,* by Richard Oster. 1987.
20. *Jerusalem, the Holy City: A Bibliography,* by James D. Purvis. Vol. I, 1988; Vol. II, 1991.
21. *An Index to English Periodical Literature on the Old Testament and Ancient Near East Studies,* by William G. Hupper. Vol. I, 1987; Vol. II, 1988; Vol. III, 1990; Vol. IV, 1990; Vol. V, 1992; Vol. VI, 1994.
22. *John and Charles Wesley: A Bibliography,* by Betty M. Jarboe. 1987.
23. *A Scholar's Guide to Academic Journals in Religion,* by James Dawsey. 1988.
24. *An Oxford Movement and Its Leaders: A Bibliography of Secondary*

and Lesser Primary Sources, by Lawrence N. Crumb. 1988; Supplement, 1993.
25. *A Bibliography of Christian Worship*, by Bard Thompson. 1989.
26. *The Disciples and American Culture: A Bibliography of Works by Disciples of Christ Members, 1866–1984*, by Leslie R. Galbraith and Heather F. Day. 1990.
27. *The Yogacara School of Buddhism: A Bibliography*, by John Powers. 1991.
28. *The Doctrine of the Holy Spirit: A Bibliography Showing Its Chronological Development* (2 vols.), by Esther Dech Schandorff. 1995.
29. *Rediscovery of Creation: A Bibliographical Study of the Church's Response to the Environmental Crisis*, by Joseph K. Sheldon. 1992.
30. *The Charismatic Movement: A Guide to the Study of Neo-Pentecostalism with Emphasis on Anglo-American Sources*, by Charles Edwin Jones. 1995.
31. *Cities and Churches: An International Bibliography* (3 vols.), by Loyde H. Hartley. 1992.
32. *A Bibliography of the Samaritans*, 2nd ed., by Alan David Crown. 1993.
33. *The Early Church: An Annotated Bibliography of Literature in English*, by Thomas A. Robinson. 1993.
34. *Holiness Manuscripts: A Guide to Sources Documenting the Wesleyan Holiness Movement in the United States and Canada*, by William Kostlevy. 1994.
35. *Of Spirituality: A Feminist Perspective*, by Clare B. Fischer. 1995.
36. *Evangelical Sectarianism in the Russian Empire and the USSR: A Bibliographic Guide*, by Albert Wardin, Jr. 1995.
37. *Hermann Sasse: A Bibliography*, by Ronald R. Feuerhahn. 1995.
38. *Women in the Biblical World: A Study Guide. Vol. I: Women in the World of Hebrew Scripture*, by Mayer I. Gruber, 1995.
39. *Women and Religion in Britain and Ireland: An Annotated Bibliography from the Reformation to 1993*, by Dale A. Johnson, 1995.
40. *Emil Brunner: A Bibliography*, by Mark G. McKim, 1996.
41. *The Book of Jeremiah: An Annotated Bibliography*, by Henry O. Thompson, 1997.

Emil Brunner
A Bibliography

by
Mark G. McKim

ATLA Bibliographies, No. 40

The Scarecrow Press, Inc.
Lanham, Md., and London

SCARECROW PRESS, INC.

Published in the United States of America
by Scarecrow Press, Inc.
4720 Boston Way
Lanham, Maryland 20706

4 Pleydell Gardens, Folkestone
Kent CT20 2DN, England

Copyright © 1996 by Mark G. McKim

All rights reserved. No part of this publication may be
reproduced, stored in a retrieval system, or transmitted
in any form or by any means, electronic, mechanical,
photocopying, recording, or otherwise, without the prior
permission of the publisher.

British Cataloguing-in-Publication Information Available

Library of Congress Cataloging-in-Publication Data

McKim, Mark G.
Emil Brunner : a bibliography / by Mark G. McKim.
 p. cm. — (ATLA bibliography series ; no. 40)
Includes index.
 1. Brunner, Emil, 1889–1966—Bibliography. 2. Neo-orthodoxy-
-Bibliography. 3. Theology, Doctrinal—History—20th century-
-Bibliography. 4. Reformed Church—Doctrines—Bibliography.
I. Title. II. Series.
Z8126.2.B67M35 1996 [BX4827 .B67] 016.23'0044'092—dc20
                                                  96-12292 CIP

ISBN 0-8108-3167-8 (cloth : alk. paper)

∞ ™ The paper used in this publication meets the minimum requirements
of American National Standard for Information Sciences—Permanence of
Paper for Printed Library Materials, ANSI Z39.48—1984.
Manufactured in the United States of America.

CONTENTS

Series Editor's Foreword	vii
Introduction	1
Acknowledgments	5
An Introduction to the Life and Thought of Emil Brunner	7
Bibliography of Emil Brunner	29
Works Written by Brunner	29
Works Edited by Brunner	73
Works Written by Brunner Jointly with Others	73
Prefaces and Forewords Written by Brunner	74
Book Reviews Written by Brunner	75
Secondary Sources: Works about Brunner	77
Index	95
About the Author	99

SERIES EDITOR'S FOREWORD

Since 1974 the American Theological Library Association has been publishing this bibliography series with the Scarecrow Press. Guidelines for projects and selections for publication are made by the ATLA Publications Section in consultation with the editor. Our goal is to stimulate and encourage the preparation and publication of reliable bibliographies and guides to the literature of religious studies in all of its scope and variety. Compilers are free to define their field, to make their own selections, and to work out internal organization as the unique demands of the subject indicate. We are pleased to publish Mark McKim's bibliography of Emil Brunner in the series.

The Reverend Doctor Mark G. McKim holds the degrees of Bachelor of Arts in history and political science from the University of New Brunswick; Master of Divinity from Acadia Divinity College, Acadia University; and Doctor of Theology from Boston University. He has published a number of scholarly and popular articles in various journals. Since 1990, Dr. McKim has served as the minister of the historic Germain Street United Baptist Church in Saint John, New Brunswick.

Kenneth E. Rowe
Series Editor

Drew University Library
Madison, NJ 07940
USA

INTRODUCTION

In preparing the bibliographies for my doctoral dissertation at Boston University, it soon became obvious that there was no complete bibliography for Emil Brunner. That lack meant compiling a large part of this present bibliography in preparation for writing my dissertation. At the encouragement of one of the theological librarians at Boston University, Stephen P. Pentek, contact was made with Dr. Ken Rowe, editor of the ATLA Bibliography Series, who readily agreed that a bibliography of Brunner was needed.

Plan and Scope

After an essay which sketches Brunner's life and major theological contributions, the bibliography is divided into three parts. The first part is a bibliography of works written by Brunner. It endeavors to cover his entire writing career. Next comes a bibliography of works about Brunner and his theological contribution. Finally, there is a subject index of Brunner's works.

Methodology

In preparing the first bibliography, works by Brunner, both existing bibliographies and various indexes and abstracting services, were searched.

The bibliographies examined were those contained in Kegley's *The Theology of Emil Brunner* and that contained in the festschrift for Brunner's sixtieth birthday, viz.—*Menschenbild im Lichte des Evangeliums Festschrift zum 60. Geburtstag von Prof. Dr. Emil Brunner*. Although there is a bibliography in the seventieth birthday festschrift, the bibliography in Kegley's book improved on it considerably as it was an updated version of the seventieth festschrift bibliography, covering the period up to 1962 while the seventieth birthday festschrift only went to 1960, and contained a special section on English language works unlike the seventieth birthday festschrift. Neither of these bibliographies however were complete.

A number of indexes and abstracting services were also consulted:

All references, for all possible variations of Brunner's name, as author, in both the *Union Theological Seminary Library Catalog* and *Missionary Research Library Catalog* were examined.

The Subject/Author volume of *Religion Index One* was searched 1949–1959 for headings Brunner (subject and author), Neo-orthodoxy (subject), and Neo-orthodox (subject). The 1949–1959 Book Review Volume was also examined. The subject and book review sections from 1960–1974 were searched manually for Brunner as author. A computer search for Brunner as author was conducted for the years 1949–59, and 1975 to the present.

A manual search of the cumulative author-editor index of *Religion Index Two* was undertaken for the years 1976–1980, under the heading "Brunner" as author-editor. A computer search for the same heading was also made for the years 1975 to the present.

The *Humanities Index* was examined for Brunner, listed as author, for the period 1974 up to March 1990. This was not examined for book reviews, as Brunner died in 1966.

Both the Rezensionenregister and Authorenregister of *Internationale Zeitschriftenschau für Bibelwissenschaft* were searched under the heading "Brunner", for the years 1951–1980 and 1987–88.

The *Cumulative Book Index* (earlier title was *United States Catalog Supplement*) was examined for Brunner as author for the period 1912 through May 1990.

The *Library of Congress Index* was manually searched in Mansell (pre-1965 imprints), and for the years 1953–1967. A computer search from 1968 to the present was also completed.

A computer search of the *Philosophers Index* was completed for the period 1940 to the present, searching for Brunner listed as author.

In preparing the second bibliography, of works about Brunner and his theology, the following sources were used:

DATRIX and the *American Doctoral Dissertation Index* were examined, beginning in 1909, and continuing to the present for dissertations under the terms Brunner, Neo-orthodox, Neo-orthodoxy.

The *Council on Graduate Studies in Religion. Doctoral Dissertations in the Field of Religion 1940–1952* was examined. This became *Dissertations: Council on Graduate Studies in Religion* which was searched for the period 1952–1967, excluding those listed under the section "in progress." The name was again changed, this time to *Council on Graduate Studies in Religion: Dissertation Title Index*, which was searched for the period 1968–1977. The most recent manifestation of the work is "Recent Dissertations in Religion" Listings in *Religious Studies Review*, which was examined for the years 1978–1990. In the 1990 numbers both "Recent Dissertations" and those listed "In Progress" were examined.

Religion Index One was searched manually in the Subject/Author Volume, under the headings: Brunner (subject *and* author), Neo-orthodox (subject), Neo-orthodoxy (subject) for 1949–1959. A manual search, under the same subject headings, was made for both the subject section and book review index for 1960–1974. The *Book Review Volume* (1949–1959) was also manually searched. A computer search for the years 1949–1959, 1975 to the present, under the three subject headings just mentioned was also conducted.

Religion Index Two was manually searched for the subject headings Brunner, Neo-orthodox and Neo-orthodoxy, for the period 1976–1980 in the Cumulative Subject Index. A computer search under the same subject headings was made for the period 1975 to the present.

The *Humanities Index* was manually searched under the same subject headings as for *Religion Index One* and *Religion Index Two* for the years 1974–March 1990. No effort was made to examine the "See Fundamentalism" references occasionally made by this index.

The *Cumulative Book Index* was searched under the same subject headings for the period from 1912–May 1990.

The *Philosophers Index* was searched by computer for the period from 1940 to the present under subject headings Neo-orthodoxy and Brunner.

The *Arts and Humanities Citation Index* was searched in a combination of computer and manual searching for the period 1975 to the present.

One published bibliography, that contained in *Emil Brunner* by J. Edward Humphrey, was also consulted.

Limitations

The bibliography excludes: manuscript indexes, audio-visual materials, and pamphlet indexes.

The first bibliography, works by Brunner, records *only* items in the original language of publication (which is most often German, but occasionally English or French) and English language translations of the item (if it was not originally in English). Hence, the bibliography records all known instances of a work in the original language of publication, and all known English translations of the same. It does not, for example, include the Hungarian language translation of *Unser Glaube* (though it does record all known editions of this work in German, the original language of publication and all known English translations of this work) nor translations *back into* German of works originally published in English.

The bibliographies do not specify a work as being a reprint unless there is an actual reference to such, or a reasonable inference may be drawn that such is the case. With some German language works, sources sometimes exhibited confusion about the terms reprint and edition, sometimes providing references such as "second *unaltered* edition" which in current North American usage would normally mean a reprint. If a source listed an item as a new edition, these bibliographies do likewise, unless there has been substantial reason to assume that instead of edition reprint was in fact meant.

Subject Index

The preparation of the subject index proved to be a daunting task. Brunner wrote on a vast array of subjects, both within and without the discipline of theology. Often, in the same article he touched on several disciplines.

The index tries to allow Brunner's writings to dictate the categories. In some instances items are listed under several categories. Occasionally, the decision as to which category or categories a piece of writing fell into had to be made somewhat arbitrarily because of the nature of the article or book. Deviations from standard indexing terms were allowed so that works could be categorized in a way that reflected their actual contents.

ACKNOWLEDGMENTS

Grateful acknowledgment is made to the following publishers for permission to quote from their copyrighted works: SCM Press Ltd., London, England; Westminster/John Knox Press, Louisville, Kentucky; Theologischer Verlag und Buchhandlungen AG Zürich, Switzerland.

I wish also to express my thanks to a number of individuals for their invaluable help in the preparation of this volume: the Reverend Doctor Jarold Zeman, retired professor of church history at Acadia Divinity College, Wolfville, Nova Scotia, Canada, who fanned a nascent interest in historical theology; the late Reverend William Zimpfer, theological librarian at Boston University and a thorough teacher in bibliographical research; Mr. Stephen Pentek, also a theological librarian at Boston University who first suggested this volume; the staff of the Ward Chipman Library at the Saint John Campus of the University of New Brunswick, especially the reference librarian, Mr. William Kerr, who became a one-man theological and church history librarian tracking down requests for the most obscure references and hard to find journals; the congregation of Germain Street United Baptist Church in Saint John, New Brunswick, Canada, which happily allowed and encouraged their pastor to devote time to this work; Mrs. Norma Bishop and Ms. Susan Greer, both deacons and members of that congregation, for their proofreading labors; Mrs. Dawn Marr, who surely heard and read more about Emil Brunner than any pastor's secretary should be expected to do; and finally my parents, Gordon and Thelma McKim, and brother, Estey McKim, for their encouragement and support.

AN INTRODUCTION TO THE LIFE AND THOUGHT OF EMIL BRUNNER

Every theologian writes within, and is inevitably influenced by a historical context. The political, economic, social, military, and personal events of the times shape theology. Indeed, it is only right that this be the case, for the task of every theologian is to present the eternal gospel to his or her contemporaries in language they can understand, and in such a manner that the gospel is seen to be relevant, intellectually defensible, important, and worthy of serious attention. This task was admirably undertaken by the late Emil Brunner.

Heinrich Emil Brunner was born near the beginning of the twentieth century, on December 23, 1889, in Winterthur, near Zurich, Switzerland. His parents were devout members of the Reformed church.

Brunner studied theology at the Universities of Berlin and Zurich, receiving his doctor of theology degree from Zurich in 1913. The previous year, he had become a minister in the Swiss Reformed Church, of which he would remain a member for the rest of his life. In 1913–14 Brunner lived in England. There he taught high school in Leeds and worked on perfecting his command of English. When the First World War broke out, Brunner returned to Switzerland, serving briefly in the militia. In 1916 he became the pastor of a small church in the mountain village of Obstalden. Here he met and married Margrit Lautenburg. The couple had four sons, the second of whom predeceased Brunner in a tragic railway accident in 1952.

Pastoral labors were interrupted during 1919 for a year of study at Union Theological Seminary in New York City. Upon his return, Brunner was appointed a Privatdozent (an unsalaried lecturer) at his alma mater in Zurich. The publication of *Die Mystik und das Wort* in 1924 secured his appointment as professor of systematic and practical theology at the University of Zurich, a position which Brunner held, with frequent interruptions for lecture tours, until 1955.

During his tenure at Zurich, Brunner was a frequent guest lecturer throughout Europe, Great Britain, and the United States. During 1938–39, for example, he was a visiting professor at Princeton Theological Seminary and at Union Seminary in New York.

In 1949 he traveled through much of Asia and the Far East. He claimed to have left part of his heart in Japan, where he returned in 1953, at age 63, to accept a teaching post as professor of christian ethics and philosophy at the International Christian University in Tokyo. Brunner wanted to be personally involved in the missionary enterprise of evangelizing Japan; however, Margrit's ill health cut their stay to only two years, and the couple returned home to Switzerland in 1955. During the ocean voyage home Brunner suffered a stroke which resulted in serious speech and physical impairment. Despite several subsequent strokes Brunner continued his theological writing which included publication of the third and final volume of his systematic theology. He died on April 6, 1966.

Major Influences on Brunner's Intellectual Development

One can trace several major influences on the development of Brunner's thought. The most significant of these occur in the period before the outbreak of World War Two, and can be seen, in one form or another, in most of Brunner's writings for the rest of his life.

Brunner always expressed gratitude for having been born into the Reformed tradition in Switzerland. In his view, the foremost influence on his thought was his Swiss nationality, of which he was intensely proud. All his life Brunner believed that the ideals of democracy and liberty were important to his thought, and he was adamantly opposed to all forms of tyranny. So permeated was his thought by these ideals, that in his popular little book *Unser Glaube* [*Our Faith*] Brunner felt it necessary to explain at some length the concept of God as king, commenting: "It is especially difficult for Swiss people to believe that we must and do have a king. The word Liberty was sung to us even in the cradle."[1] Again, his whole theological production was shaped, guided, and molded by the Reformed tradition. One of Brunner's grandfathers was a

Reformed minister and his parents were both devout believers from that tradition. Brunner was born near Zurich, the site of Ulrich Zwingli's labors, and he pastored in the canton of Glarus, in which, five hundred years earlier, Zwingli had also served. This initial Reformed influence was intensified by his later studies in the circle loosely centered around Karl Barth.

The pastoral experience, combined with extensive travel abroad, may have been responsible for Brunner's becoming what might be termed a "practical" systematic theologian. At the University of Zurich, for example, Brunner's position was that of professor of both practical *and* systematic theology. Brunner contended that he was above all else a preacher of the Good News. Unlike some theologians who practiced their craft for its own sake and lost themselves in endless journal debates, Brunner believed that the work of the systematic theologian was of value only if it helped people to understand the gospel and facilitated its communication to the world. "Real theology," as he put it, "is not only for experts, but it is for all to whom religious questions are also problems of thought."[2] This view is seen very clearly in Brunner's writing, which often gives helpful illustrations to make a point. And when Brunner defined faith in terms of trusting obedience, he sometimes resorted to a hyperbolic emphasis on the obedience part of the definition to the extent one might assume that he was turning faith into performance of good works! That was not what was being taught. Rather, it appears in his insistence on the practicality of faith, his words betrayed him!

The religious socialist movement was also an important and potent influence on Brunner's thought. (One should note, incidentally, the practical orientation of this movement.) With its great sympathy for the needs of the working class, the movement reached Switzerland through the work of two German Lutheran pastor-evangelists, Johann Christoph Blumhardt (1805–1880), and his son, Christoph Blumhardt (1842–1919). The pair gave the movement, in contrast to its original theologically liberal German context, a much more conservative foundation. It had strongly pietistic origins. Although Brunner knew Christoph Blumhardt personally, the Blumhardts' influence on him was mainly indirect and came through two Swiss Christian Socialists, Hermann Kutter (1863–1931) under whom Brunner was catechized, and Leonhard Ragaz (1868–1945), one of Brunner's professors at Zurich. A considerable number of Brunner's writings over the years show marked interest in social, economic, and political issues.

The fourth element in Brunner's intellectual development was his being drawn during the 1920s into the small circle of theologians loosely centered around Karl Barth. The group was by no means uniform, nor was it a society dedicated to the admiration of Barth. What united the individuals in it was a shared disillusionment brought on by the devastation of World War One and a common belief that theological liberalism had been shown to be bankrupt. Brunner, like the others in the group, had been trained in the classical liberal tradition, but long before he joined this group—indeed, while he had been a pastor in Glarus—a profound change in his views had begun. In fact, as early as 1914 in his *Das Symbolische in der Religiösen* Brunner had been consciously trying to get beyond Schleiermacher, and he severely criticized him in his 1924 book, *Die Mystik und das Wort*. As this loose knit group of scholars made an intensive study first of Luther, then of Calvin, Brunner became convinced that although important insights into what the Bible taught had been recovered by the first Reformers, such understanding had been lost by subsequent generations of Protestants. This, he came to believe, was particularly true with regard to the nature of faith. Brunner believed that much of his work was merely the restoring of the biblical message which the Reformers had recovered.

The school of thought developed by this group was variously called "theology of crisis," "dialectical theology," "neo-orthodox," and "Barthian theology." Brunner objected to the last name, undoubtedly because the direction of his own theology had already been determined before he encountered Karl Barth. In his review of Barth's *Commentary on Romans* (1919), which had brought the new school to the world's attention, Brunner was highly complimentary. He insisted nevertheless that the book was a confirmation of his own thought, not that it had originated his position. Brunner steadfastly maintained that he had arrived at his views independently of Barth, and during the 1930s this independence was highlighted in a dispute between the two over natural theology.

During this period three factors were particularly important in Brunner's continuing development.

The first was the Oxford Group Movement established in England by F. N. D. Buchman. As ever, deeply interested in the practical, Brunner saw potential in this movement for revitalizing the church, particularly the laity, and for reaching those whom the institutional church was not touching. He took a role in the house meetings and Bible study groups, and published a short and highly readable book on the relationship between the church and the Oxford Group Movement.

The second factor influencing Brunner during this period was his serious introduction to Søren Kierkegaard through the writings of Martin Buber and his I-Thou philosophy. In his writings Brunner is often highly complimentary of both men, particularly Kierkegaard. Their writings helped Brunner to work out his anthropology. He concluded that our humanity consisted in our ability or potential to have an intimate relationship with the Creator. From this understanding of humanity Brunner went on to deal with what was perhaps the most central question of his theology: the nature of truth—in particular, how did the Bible understand the nature of truth. Heavily influenced by Kierkegaard, Brunner concluded that in the Scripture truth was always "truth as encounter." Real truth always changed the individual involved. It was not objective, "out there," to be controlled or manipulated.

The final aspect to Brunner's development during the 1930s stemmed from his stormy controversy with Karl Barth over the question of natural theology. Both men were agreed that an independent natural theology was impossible. Contrary to Roman Catholic teaching, unaided human reason could not attain to clear knowledge of God, nor demonstrate God's existence by means of logical proofs.

Nevertheless, Brunner believed that some very limited capacity remained, despite sin, for humans to hear and understand the gospel. The image of God in humanity had not been completely destroyed by the fall in that the "formal" aspect of the image, that is, the capacity to recognize God and to have an intimate relationship with God, remained intact. Because the formal image had not been destroyed, we remain human, and can be held responsible for our sin; the "material" aspect of the image, the actual and correct functioning of this capacity, was destroyed. Moreover, Brunner believed that something of God is revealed in nature. Nature was God's creation, and it could not help but demonstrate something about God. Some knowledge of God, though clearly insufficient for a personal "encounter" with God, could be had by observing creation. It should be noted that, here again, Brunner's emphasis on the practical is apparent. Theology, in his view, had to have some "point of contact" with fallen humanity, to enable the missionary and apologetic endeavor to proceed. If humanity was completely blinded by sin, and utterly unable to see anything of God in the natural world, what point was there for preaching, apologetic endeavor, or missionary outreach?

Brunner set forth these views in a short essay entitled *Natur und Gnade* [*Nature and Grace*] in 1934. Barth responded shortly with his vitriolic *Nein!* [*No!*]. Barth saw any form of natural theology, even Brunner's extremely limited variety, as unacceptable. He chastised Brunner, claiming that, in his system, humans were seen as having some role in their own salvation. In fact this was not what Brunner had written, and there is some question whether Barth fully understood Brunner's argument.

The essential difference between the two was that Barth insisted there was no revelation whatever outside of Jesus Christ. Only his miraculous inbreaking into the life of an unbeliever was revelatory. There was no "point of contact" except from God's side. Brunner on the other hand believed that there was legitimate revelation of God outside Christ, though it was by no means sufficient to bring an individual to the point of submission and surrender to God. In his later writing, perhaps influenced by his travels in the East, Brunner elaborated on this theme. He argued that any religion, however obscure or bizarre, if it called on men and women to abandon their false self-autonomy, was to that degree true, and drew those men and women toward the true faith.

Major Themes and Emphases in Brunner's Theology

Given Brunner's extraordinarily long and prolific writing career, as well as some changes in his views over the years, one must approach the responsibility of summarizing the major themes in his work with fear and trembling!

Certain boundaries must inevitably be set in any effort at summary. In the present instance, the rich mine of social and political commentary and reflection must, regrettably, be left untapped, that one may attempt some overview of Brunner's major theological views. In a sense, this is being faithful to Brunner himself, for whom prolegomena were so important. His social and political views were deeply rooted in his theology.

Given that Brunner was consciously rejecting the inadequacies of classical liberal theology, it should come as no surprise that he devoted much of his work to foundational issues in theology. In a sense post–World War One theology had to be rebuilt from the foundations up. This emphasis on foundational theological issues is seen in the attention Brunner gave to five issues: the nature of truth and the closely related issue of the nature of faith, the relationship of revelation and reason, the questions of natural theology and humanity's capacity to respond to God, and the person and work of Jesus Christ.

The Nature of Truth

To Brunner, the tragedy of much contemporary theology was that it was controlled by a dichotomy dividing truth into subjective and objective spheres. Brunner believed this "subject-object thesis" was foreign to the biblical understanding of truth, and when applied to theology distorted the nature of truth.

Since the Enlightenment, humans had seen themselves as the subjects who investigated various objects. Objective thinkers, such as scientists, valued highly their ability to let the facts of their research or tests speak for themselves. But when applied to theology, objectivistic thought meant that humanity was trying to control the subject of investigation, God. That is why Brunner in *Our Faith* [*Unser glaube*] wrote in answer to the opening question "Is there a God?":

> To the merely inquisitive question, 'Is there a God?' I should be interested to know if there is one . . . perhaps one should reply . . . No, there is no God. 'There is a Himalaya range, there is a planet Uranus, there is an element radium . . . but there is no God. God is neither an object of scientific investigation nor something that we can insert in the treasure of our knowledge, as one mounts a rare stamp' . . . If your question were answered 'Yes there is a God,' you would depart with one more illusion, for you would then suppose that God is in a class with other objects.[3]

God in other words, is not an object which can be manipulated or controlled.

On the other hand, subjective thinking, which Brunner certainly considered the lesser of the two evils, tended, over against objectivism, to make truth into something which one found inwardly.

Truth became a "toffee nose" with every individual his own final authority in matters of faith and practice.

Brunner contended that truth in the biblical sense was always "truth as encounter." Truth, in Scripture, was always God's encounter of a human being. This truth always, in some fashion, changed the recipient of that truth.

The Nature of Faith

Brunner's understanding of faith can perhaps best be understood by delineating what he believed it was not. For Brunner there were two equally erroneous concepts of faith. One of them, tied to the understanding of truth as objective, he described variously as "orthodoxy," "objectivism," "scholasticism," and "theologismus." The other, tied to the understanding of truth as subjective, Brunner called "subjectivism" and "pietism." Of the two, Brunner clearly considered the first to be the more serious and the most prevalent.[4]

The hallmark of orthodoxy[5] according to Brunner was an overwhelming emphasis on correctness of belief. This emphasis occurred because to orthodoxy, faith was a manner of mental assent to, or intellectual agreement with, right doctrinal statements. Brunner believed that among Roman Catholics such assent took the form of belief in an infallible pope, whereas with Protestants the assent was belief in a Bible infallible in all areas, even those not pertaining to matters of faith and practice.

Orthodoxy, according to Brunner, was not faithful to the biblical witness on several counts. Its objectivistic conception of truth as something "out there" to be grasped showed the human tendency to try to bring things, in this case, God, under human control, subject to human manipulation.[6] Brunner contended that God was never an object for human control, but rather the eternal subject. Orthodoxy was also an error because it made faith into a human work, when, according to Scripture, faith is God's gift.[7] As Brunner wrote: "Correct doctrine is something that can be learned, and indeed anyone who has a good brain and is able to study at a good college or university can learn it easily. But faith is not something that a man can 'learn'; it is the free gift of God."[8] Brunner believed that the orthodox view of faith turned something which was God's gift into "a human achievement, a *sacrificium intellectus*."[9] Finally, orthodoxy was an error because in the New Testament "the object of faith was Jesus Christ himself, and not merely some doctrine *about* [italics mine] him."[10] As Brunner himself put it "Faith is not relation to a doctrine, to that which ought to be believed, but it is the obedience of faith . . . to Jesus Christ himself."[11]

On the other hand, to Brunner, pietism, though not so widespread an error, was also incorrect in its understanding of faith. The notion that there could be any sort of genuine faith devoid—or virtually devoid—of content was abhorrent to him. Reacting against the classical liberal theology of his youth, Brunner claimed that "faith is certainly not the 'pious feeling' of 'absolute dependence'."[12] Brunner believed that doctrine was absolutely necessary, and even described doctrine as "der Grund des Galubens."[13] Without a certain amount of doctrine, genuine faith was impossible. As he put it:

> a certain amount of doctrine must be present before living faith can come into being. Of course this can be an extraordinarily small amount. The jailer was changed in one night from a pagan into a believer. This conversion manifestly took place with a minimum of doctrine; the same obtained with those 'three thousand souls' who on Pentecost 'were added'.[14]

It was, for Brunner, nonsensical to suppose that faith could occur without some amount of knowledge, for humans could not grasp the content, the reality, of the personal self-giving of God without some framework of doctrine.[15]

One had to go beyond the extremes of both orthodoxy and pietism, Brunner argued, to find truly biblical faith.[16] The right understanding of faith was to be found, not so much between these two extremes as in a paradox which involved both yet also transcended both.[17] This paradoxical concept of faith was closely tied to Brunner's understanding of what truth meant in the biblical sense.

Because any attempt to understand spiritual truth by means of the object-subject thesis was wrong, its application to understanding faith was a disaster which falsified faith.[18] Truth in the biblical sense was always truth as encounter, truth which changed the recipient of that truth. Just so, faith could not be simply mental assent to a propositional statement, because such faith would not change the person who so assents. Rather "faith is not a relation to 'something', to an idea . . . a doctrine . . . but it is wholly a personal relationship: my trustful obedience to Him who meets me as the gracious Lord."[19] Since unbelief in the biblical perspective is not refusal to accept certain propositions so much as an assertion of the individual's will to autonomy over against God,[20] the opposite of unbelief is "faith . . . the cessation of the false independence of man and his return to the original attitude of dependence."[21] For Brunner, genuine faith is understood in personal terms, as a relationship of trusting obedience (*vertrauensgehorsam*) to God in Jesus Christ.

This understanding of faith does not mean that doctrine has no place, or that Brunner slips into the fideism of the sort that he himself decries. In Brunner's scheme, doctrine has a crucial, but always secondary, position. It serves to guide or point one in the right direction, so that faith is placed in the right object, Jesus Christ. Doctrinal belief is the vehicle for faith. Indeed "The majority of those who in the past have proved themselves genuine believers . . . came by way of the Church catechism to this faith."[22] The important point for Brunner was that doctrine was secondary to faith, understood as a relationship of trusting obedience to Jesus Christ.

Revelation and Reason

Brunner defined revelation as "something hidden . . . [being] made known."[23] Revelation meant that something which would otherwise remain hidden from human sight, became known. Revelation was in fact a way of obtaining knowledge that is radically different from the usual methods, such as empirical investigation. But, in line with his understanding of the nature of truth, Brunner maintained that what was revealed was not a set of doctrinal propositions, but rather God.

Brunner vehemently disagreed with Barth who believed that there was only one type of revelation—in Christ. God, argued Brunner, has provided a general revelation, which though it is not salvific, is quite sufficient to show humanity its sinfulness, make it culpable, and demonstrate something of God's majesty. Even other world religions in some sense point humanity toward God, though Brunner saw them as often very mixed with sin. The culmination of God's self-revelation was certainly in Jesus Christ, and this revelation not only has saving significance but opens human eyes to God's revelation elsewhere, such as, in nature.

There are, contended Brunner, several witnesses to God's primary self-revelation, including the sacraments, the church as a community of believers, and good works. Each witness in one way or another points to Christ. For Brunner, however, it is the Bible, and the internal witness of the Holy Spirit which are the most important witnesses to God's revelation. The Bible must not be thought of as being the revelation itself, but rather the primary witness to and the primary record of that revelation. Hence, it is the norm for all Christian teaching and preaching. The Holy Spirit is the one who opens the eyes of the unbeliever, revealing Christ directly. Brunner argued that a Christian acknowledged Christ as Lord because of this direct convincement, not because one had been rationally argued into belief in the reliability of the Scriptures, and then went from there to accept what the authors had written about Jesus. Rather, the Holy Spirit convinces one inwardly of the identity of Jesus, and the authority of the Scriptures.

Keenly aware that critics demanded rational proof of Christian beliefs, Brunner argued that this experience of the internal witness of the spirit was epistemologically valid knowledge. It was not the same as rational knowledge, but it was, nevertheless, just as valid. Brunner was in fact rejecting the claim from the Enlightenment that the only valid form of knowledge was the empirical. Reason was only one of several ways of knowing, and a secondary way at that. Hence, the title of Brunner's work, *Revelation and Reason*.

These two ways of knowing were, said Brunner, both valid. But they provided different kinds of knowledge. Revelation provides knowledge which is personal, is gained only when an individual surrenders to God, and is life-changing. It is the sort of knowledge which can never be obtained by reason alone. Reason on the other hand provides impersonal knowledge, or a knowledge of some object. This sort of knowledge makes no particular moral change in the individual who receives it. The two forms of knowledge are complementary, each having its own particular field. Problems begin when one oversteps the bounds into the field of the other, a situation particularly noticeable in the long running, and in Brunner's view, usually foolish, harmful, and unnecessary battle between science and theology.

It is when reason turns into rationalism, claiming to be the only valid means of knowing, in fact taking over God's place, that there is conflict with the knowledge received by means of faith, as a result of revelation.[24]

"Reason," as Brunner put it, "is right wherever it listens to the Word of God, and does not think that it is able to proclaim the divine truth to itself."[25]

Natural Theology and Human Capacity

The questions of whether there is any revelation outside of Christ, and whether humanity has any capacity to respond to God's revelation, in or outside of Christ, are closely intertwined in Brunner's thought.

Brunner argued forcefully that there was a general, or natural, revelation, that is to say, that something of God could be known from creation. In this view, he parted company with Karl Barth who insisted that the only revelation of God was to be found in Christ.

Brunner gave two major arguments for the existence of a general revelation in nature. The first and most strongly put of these arguments was Brunner's contention that such a general revelation in nature was crucial to establishing and maintaining human responsibility. In God's eyes, humanity was guilty, but humanity could only be fairly judged guilty if it were responsible, and it could only be responsible if there was some revelation to which it might respond, or fail to respond.[26] Essentially Brunner here is echoing the apostle Paul's argument that where there is no law, there can be no sin.[27] Brunner put it forcefully, commenting: ". . . the Bible expects us to consider this revelation through the Creation . . . to ignore it is condemned as the great sin of the heathen; likewise it is evident that the Bible bases the responsibility of all men . . . upon the possibility of knowing him [God], given by God himself [through the general revelation]."[28] Continuing to parallel Paul's argument that all humanity is guilty, having failed to respond to the revelation in nature,[29] Brunner comments, "Men are held guilty because they do not recognize this revelation so clearly in front of them."[30] Worse still, "man misrepresents this revelation and turns it into idols."[31] Second, Brunner argued that just as one can learn something of any artist by considering his or her work, Scripture logically concludes that one could also know something of God's nature from looking at God's handiwork.[32]

Having labored hard and long to establish that there was indeed a general revelation in nature, Brunner however was equally concerned to set out its limitations. The general revelation had its purpose, but it was not salvific. There was not enough in it to bring humans back into a right relationship of trusting obedience to God, nor would it tell one much about God's loving concern for the human sinner, nor was there any provision in it for dealing with sin. Worse still, "sin [even] prevents man from seeing this revelation through the Creation aright."[33] In the end, it demanded God's direct inbreaking into the human situation, in Christ, to save humanity.

The important question for Brunner, then, became whether humanity had any capacity to respond to God's revelation. In traditional Reformed thought the answer to that was resoundingly negative. The fall so damaged humanity that no capacity for response remained. Only if, out of the mass of perdition, God, from all eternity past, had elected an individual to be saved, did that individual have his or her spiritual eyes opened, and receive the gift of repentance and faith. Any suggestion that humanity participated in the process in any fashion was condemned as works righteousness, a dilution of the doctrine of *sola gratia*. As for the rest of humanity, it stood under the divine decree of damnation, having been selected by God from all eternity for that fate.

Brunner rejected this notion of double predestination, which, in his view, robbed humanity of all responsible decision, and meant that indeed humans had no capacity whatever to respond to God's self-revelation. He based that rejection on several points, which here can be sketched only in brief. If God had predetermined from eternity who would be saved and damned, in fact creating some for the sole purpose of being damned, then God's nature as love was brought into serious question.[34] It would be "impossible truly to worship this God as the God of love."[35] Moreover, if God was the absolute author of all things, it would make him the author of sin, a conclusion which Zwingli drew, but which Calvin recoiled from with the less than satisfactory explanation that one must not draw such a conclusion.[36] Furthermore, the question would be begged "what use is it to preach the Gospel and to call men to repentance? He who is going to be saved will be saved in any case, and he who is doomed . . . will in any case be lost."[37] Why should Scripture command us to summon people to make a decision about God, when in fact the decision is really just an illusion—no real decision at all?[38]

But Brunner's strongest argument against double predestination came back to the question of whether humanity could respond to God's revelation or not. If the traditional Reformed view was correct, then "there could be neither freedom nor responsibility . . . since everything has already been decided in eternity."[39] Humanity was nothing more than a puppet, an automaton. Yet to Brunner, Scripture clearly taught that responsibility to God was the distinguishing feature of humanity. Our humanity consisted in our having been created in God's image; that is, we were created to live in a responsible, intimate relationship of trusting obedience to God. Even though as sinners we do not actually live in this way, we can never evade the responsibility to do so. But in the usual Reformed scheme, humanity was reduced to the level of puppets, whose response to God or lack thereof had been determined in advance by God. Humans could not be held responsible for their response under such circumstances. They had no choice about their response. It had been made for them. Therefore, there had to be something seriously wrong with the usual Reformed explanation!

Humanity, Brunner argued, is called to responsible decision, for or against God's lordship, and that decision, if humanity is not to be reduced to puppet status, must be a real decision, with real consequences. God accepts the yes as a real yes, and the no as a real no. "Faith is decision in which the stakes are salvation or ruin; it is not a sham decision, where everything has already been decided beforehand."[40]

Brunner believed that one had to hold in creative tension the two paradoxical beliefs—that salvation was solely a matter of God's grace, and at the same time, that humanity was called to make a real decision for or against God. How the two could be reconciled was a mystery beyond human understanding, and beyond the scope of Scripture. Theological speculation about how the two could be reconciled frequently led to less than desirable results which either turned humanity into puppets and God into a heartless tyrant, or at the other extreme, suggested that humanity was partly responsible for its own salvation, and thus denied the doctrine of *sola gratia*.

Jesus Christ

Brunner's theology was unreservedly and pronouncedly christocentric. He dismissed critics who objected Christian theology should be theocentric instead, pointing out this objection failed to take into account that a Christ-centered theology was, by definition, also God centered, for who else was Christ but God come among humanity?[41] Behind Brunner's conviction that Christian theology had to be christocentric was the belief that God was made known to humanity most clearly in Christ. While something of God could be known in nature, and through conscience, it was only in Christ that a clear picture of what God is like emerged. Closely related to this was Brunner's conviction that only in Christ was humanity confronted in an unavoidable fashion with "the decision" for or against God's claim to be absolute Lord of the individual's life.[42] Indeed, running throughout all Brunner's work is the abiding conviction that the real issue facing humanity is their deciding for or against Christ's claim to lordship. He argued that being a Christian meant nothing more or less than confessing with the first Christians, "Jesus is Lord." As he wrote:

> The first Christian confession of faith ran thus: Christ the Lord. To believe means to have a Lord, a King, who really, that is unconditionally, without restriction, is King, an absolute Lord with no democracy. The meaning of revelation is the dethronement of the self, the rebel, by the rightful monarch.[43]

For Brunner everything beyond this most basic confession of faith was frosting on the cake, a working out of this confession.

Brunner gave substantial attention to the person and work of Christ in both his magnificent volume, *Das Mittler* [*The Mediator*], and his later three-volume systematic theology. The major change between the two treatments was that in his systematic theology, Brunner reversed the order from *Das Mittler*, where he had followed the traditional pattern of dealing first with the person and then the work of Christ. He did so on the grounds that we come to understand who Christ is on the basis of what he does, not the other way around. More important though is that in his discussion of both the work and person of Christ, Brunner not only broke decisively with classical liberal theology, but strongly criticized its view of the person of Christ.

Friedrich Schleiermacher had in all essential points set out the view of Christ held by classical liberal theologians. He was heavily influenced by the criticisms raised by the Enlightenment against any claims of uniqueness or exclusiveness for or by Christ. As the great age of sail and exploration had opened up new continents and brought the discovery of new world religions, philosophes like Voltaire had questioned and ridiculed the traditional Christian claim that Christ was the only way of salvation. They claimed to perceive a common denominator in all religion, focused on ethical practice; everything beyond that could and should be jettisoned. Schleiermacher was certainly conscious of such criticisms. In both *The Christian Faith*, and more particularly in *On Religion: Speeches to its Cultured Despisers*, he tried to play the role of an apologist, but in his effort to do so he virtually adopted whole the Enlightenment position. Schleiermacher took the view that the essence of all religion was not ethics, but what he called the feeling of "absolute dependence" upon God. More than anyone else in history, Jesus expressed and had this experience. In that sense, and that sense alone, could Jesus be called divine. He was not the unique, divine, Son of God in the traditional understanding. Christianity and its founder therefore were superior to other world religions and teachers in degree only. Christ was not to be seen as God's special and final revelation to humanity. There was in fact no special revelation at all, only a general revelation available to all men and women. Equally there were many great teachers who helped others understand this general revelation and its essential point of "absolute dependence," though admittedly Christ was the best such teacher who had been cast up by history to date.

Against this view, Brunner took direct and devastating aim. To begin, he pointed out that Schleiermacher had been inconsistent in his views; for while arguing that the general revelation, or universal religion, was based on feeling, not knowledge, he agreed that Christianity was based on a knowable historical person, Christ! Yet if this was so, Brunner pointed out, then using Schleiermacher's own definition of the universal religion as something being based on feeling, Christianity could not be part of it.[44]

But even more pointed was Brunner's contention that there was an absolute dividing line on this issue. "It is," he wrote, "impossible to combine the Christian Faith with this belief in a universal religion . . . we must choose one side or the other; there is no middle path."[45] Bluntly, whether some consider it intolerant or not, the heart of the Christian faith is the belief in a specific revelation and one mediator.[46] Jesus, argued Brunner, was unique, not because he was the bearer of revelation—there have been many such—but because he was the revelation; not a creature like us, but one who comes from the divine side of the creature/creator boundary.[47] "That which we . . . see in Christ," he wrote, "is absolutely nothing other than God . . ."[48] Whereas a prophet was but a messenger who claimed to bring a word from God, Jesus claimed to be the message itself, the Word of God, and was clearly portrayed in Scripture as fully divine and fully human. To confess Jesus as Lord, which Brunner contended was what made one a Christian, meant to acknowledge Jesus as rightful and absolute master of one's life, and who but the Creator-God himself could make such a claim on a human life?

Brunner was equally adamant in his treatment of the work of Christ. Enlightenment-influenced theologians, he wrote, believed that the real human problem was merely a misunderstanding—that we erroneously perceive God as a judge.[49] In fact, Brunner said, Scripture teaches that the Christian faith is not about dealing with a mere misunderstanding, which in the end can never be that serious; the consequences of "the problem" are dreadfully serious; therefore, the problem, whatever it may be, must be serious too.[50] That problem is sin, the human decision to rebel against the rightful sovereign Lord. That affront to the divine honor, and God's will to be Lord, separates humanity from God, and subjects it to God's wrath. However unpopular the notion that ". . . the holy God will punish disobedient humanity with final and absolute ruin,"[51] God's holiness, taking self seriously, which in turn gives seriousness and meaning to everything else, demands just that response to rebellion. The work of Christ, therefore, was not about showing humans how they had misguidedly concluded that God was a judge. His work and mission was to do something to avert the carrying out of the divine sentence, and to restore humanity to a relationship of trusting obedience to God. While Brunner clearly understood and readily acknowledged that moderns found the whole notion of atonement difficult to understand, he also believed that to turn Christ into a teacher who helped misguided pupils was a complete misrepresentation of who Christ was, and what he was about.

Evaluation of Brunner's Life and Influence

There is a popular notion that Brunner was merely the mouthpiece for Karl Barth. This is as unfortunate as it is untrue. Granted the two men had much in common. They shared a devotion to the task of reconstructing theology from the ruins of classical liberalism. The Christian message had to be rescued alike from classical liberalism and sterile, mindless "orthodoxy." The former had swallowed much of the Enlightenment and most of the supposedly assured results of higher criticism, and had turned Jesus into a religious genius but certainly not God incarnate, the eternal Word, the Lord. The latter, in virtually ignoring the Enlightenment, and the impressive results of modern scientific methods and investigations, had made it seem that no educated person could be a believer.

Brunner was however an independent thinker differing from Barth in a number of ways. Of course their famous—or infamous—dispute about natural theology and human capacity is only one such area of difference. There were others. Barth has been called the "theologian's theologian," his writing being heavily academic. Brunner, though no less academically qualified, had an easier style in his writings and lectures, and deliberately tried to make systematic theology serve a practical end. He believed strongly that the purpose of systematic theology was to make the message of the gospel clear to each new generation. In Barth's writing there was a tendency to be unconcerned that Scripture be objectively true, or historically accurate. The reader is left to ponder how something could be subjectively true, verified by the inner witness of the Holy Spirit, but possibly objectively false. Rudolf Bultmann derived this tendency from Barth, combined it with his skepticism about the historical accuracy of the New Testament records, and created an almost complete break between the Christ of faith and the Christ of history. Brunner, on the other hand, perhaps because of his belief in the possibility of a limited natural theology, was far less prone to this separation of the historical truth from that derived from revelation. While Christian faith and its inward certainty could not be based on the results of historical investigation, there was—and in the end there never could be—a contradiction between the results of unbiased historical investigation and that which was known by faith.

During his own lifetime Brunner was recognized as a major figure in the theological enterprise, of which he was in the forefront for almost four decades. His significance was recognized with several honorary degrees from universities in Europe, Great Britain, and the United States. Brunner was not only the first to introduce neo-orthodoxy to the English speaking world, but he traveled and taught in Britain and the United States more frequently than any other major European exponent of the new movement. Indeed, during its early years he was the only widely known exponent in the English speaking world. Two generations of seminary students cut their theological teeth on the writings of Emil Brunner.

Brunner was proud of his Reformed heritage, but in his writing did not shrink from criticism of any theological position, even in his own tradition, which he believed was a deviation from the biblical norm. For example, he ended up essentially rejecting infant baptism, practiced in the Swiss Reformed Church, on the grounds that it required no personal faith on the part of the baptized infant.

Although proud of his Reformed heritage, Brunner was heavily involved in the ecumenical movement. This included not only his active involvement in the Oxford Group Movement, but also participation in discussions leading to the formation of the World Council of Churches in 1948.

Barth and Brunner died within two years of one another, depriving the neo-orthodox movement of its leading lights. The health of the movement was also hurt by Rudolf Bultmann who borrowed heavily from Barth, but took a radically skeptical approach to Scripture which was not in line with either Barth's or Brunner's views. These and other factors meant that neo-orthodoxy did not long survive the deaths of its leading lights as a separate school of thought within Protestantism. In a sense the movement suffered from being too liberal for conservative theologians, and too conservative for liberals. The left decried the attack on its view of the person and work of Christ, and the high view of the authority of Scripture which neo-orthodoxy took. The far right feared any attempt to deal with the criticisms raised during and after the Enlightenment as concessions to modernism. Since the deaths of Barth and Brunner, Protestant theology has generally lacked great systematizers and has been increasingly fragmented. Moreover, the numerous and competing schools in the theological enterprise—from black, feminist, and process theology to liberation and ecofeminist theology—often seem to be more discussions about ethics than systematic theology.

Nevertheless, through his writings, Brunner continues to exercise a considerable influence: articles, dissertations, and theses continue to appear dealing with one aspect or another of Brunner's thought, some of his most popular and influential books are in recent reprint, and theologians as diverse as Reinhold Niehbuhr and Dale Moody have been clearly impacted by Brunner.

Can it be argued that Brunner has any place in today's theological enterprise, or is he to be relegated to commentaries on historical theology? That depends on what one thinks Protestant theology should be doing in the late twentieth century.

If the job of theology is to take eternal truths, and present them in such a fashion as makes a serious effort to take into account the philosophical and scientific knowledge, views, opinions, and criticisms of its era, then Brunner still has a role to play. In a very real sense, Brunner saw the theologian's job as taking the eternal good news, and setting it out in terms relevant to modern, post-Enlightenment men and women.

If theology is more than articles in journals read only by experts; if theology is intended to be a servant of the church and its mission; if the hope of every theologian and pastor is to be called a theologian-pastor; if in the end theology is supposed to serve the practical task of explaining the Christian faith to the average man or woman, then Brunner is still relevant.

If Protestant theology decides that ecumenicity means more than ecclesiastical snuggling together in a cold world, but rather working together because of a common confession of Christ as Lord, and agreement on the deepest spiritual questions, Brunner still has something to say.

And if in an increasingly secularized world there is still need for a restatement, reformulation, and reaffirmation of the cardinal points of the Reformation, the origins of Protestant theology, Brunner is still relevant: *sola fide, sola gratia, sola scriptura, solus Christus, sola deo gloria.*

Notes

1. Emil Brunner, *Our Faith*, 2nd ed., trans. John W. Rilling (London: SCM Press Ltd., 1936; reprint, London: SCM Press Ltd., 1949), 66 (page references are to reprint edition).

2. Emil Brunner, *Man in Revolt*, trans. Olive Wyon (Philadelphia: Westminster Press, 1947), 11.

3. *Our Faith*, 13.

4. As far as Brunner was concerned the objectivistic error had progressed to such a degree that it was to be seen in more than just an incorrect understanding of faith. Brunner believed that the church had, as a result of

this error, come to be viewed as an institution, a dispenser of sacraments, rather than an assembly of believers. He insisted on distinguishing one from the other by referring to the institution as "church" but the assembly as "ekklesia". Furthermore, Brunner thought that the objectivistic error had corrupted a right understanding of the sacraments. Hence he condemned infant baptism because it involved no personal response on the part of the individual being baptized, and equally criticized the *ex opere operata* interpretation of communion which had turned grace into an automatic operation.

5. Brunner uses the term in a broad sense, not primarily with reference to the 17th-century movement of the same name.

6. Emil Brunner, *Truth as Encounter*, trans. Amandus W. Loos, David Cairns, T. H. L. Parker, enlgd. ed. of *The Divine-Human Encounter* (Philadelphia: Westminster Press, 1964), 167.

7. Emil Brunner, *Revelation and Reason: The Christian Doctrine of Faith and Knowledge*, trans. Olive Wyon (1946; reprint, Wake Forest, N.C.: Chanticleer Publishing Company, Inc., n.d.), 420.

8. Ibid.

9. Ibid., 183, 184.

10. J. Edward Humphrey, *Emil Brunner*, Makers of the Modern Theological Mind Series (Waco, Texas: Word Books, 1976), 127.

11. Emil Brunner, *The Christian Doctrine of God*, Dogmatics I. trans. Olive Wyon (Philadelphia: Westminster Press, 1950; reprint, Philadelphia: Westminster Press, 1980), 106, 107.

12. Ibid., 61.

13. Emil Brunner, *Dogmatik*, vol. 3, *Die Christliche Lehre von der Kirche vom Glauben and von der Vollendung* (Zurich: Zwingli-Verlag, 1960), 192.

14. *Truth as Encounter*, 140.

15. Ibid., 132–34.

16. Ibid., 84.

17. Ibid., 84, 85.

18. Ibid., 69.

19. *Revelation and Reason*, 36.

20. Humphrey, 125.

21. Emil Brunner, *The Mediator: A Study of the Central Doctrine of the Christian Faith*, trans. Olive Wyon (Philadelphia: Westminster Press, 1947), 609.

22. Emil Brunner, *The Christian Doctrine of the Church, Faith and the Consummation*, Dogmatics III. trans. David Cairns, T. H. L. Parker (Philadelphia: Westminster Press, 1962), 241.

23. *Revelation and Reason*, 23.

24. *Man in Revolt*, 244.

25. Ibid.

26. Emil Brunner and Karl Barth, *Natural Theology Comprising "Nature and Grace" by Professor Dr. Emil Brunner and the reply "No!" by Dr. Karl Barth*, trans. Peter Fraenkel (London: Geoffrey Bles: the Centenary Press, 1946), 11.
27. Romans 4.15.
28. *Man in Revolt*, 529, 530.
29. Romans 1.18–23, 3.9–18
30. *Natural Theology*, 25.
31. Ibid., 26.
32. Ibid., 24.
33. *Man in Revolt*, 530
34. *The Christian Doctrine of God*, 306.
35. Ibid., 331.
36. Ibid., 331, 332.
37. Ibid., 333.
38. Ibid., 333.
39. Ibid., 332.
40. Ibid., 314, 315.
41. Emil Brunner, *The Mediator: A Study of the Central Doctrine of the Christian Faith*, trans. Olive Wyon (Philadelphia: Westminster Press, 1947), 400.
42. Ibid., 586.
43. Ibid., 585, 586.
44. Ibid., 55.
45. Ibid., 71.
46. Ibid.
47. Ibid., 240, 241.
48. Ibid., 401.
49. Ibid., 486.
50. Ibid., 488, 489.
51. Ibid., 464.

BIBLIOGRAPHY OF EMIL BRUNNER

Works Written by Brunner

1. "D'Abord la règne de Dieu. Trad. libre et abgrégée d'une prédication à Thoune au mois d'âout, lors d'une réunion nationale des groupes d'Oxford." ?Translated by Charles Béguin. *Les Cahiers Protestants* 18 (1934).
2. "The Absoluteness of Jesus." Translated by Vernon S. Broyles, Jr. *Union Seminary Review* 46 (July 1935): 269–82.
3. "Abrahams Glaube. Predigt." *Extemis, cahiers périodiques* 3 (1937).
4. "Die Absolutheit Jesus." In *Vorträge geh. auf der 29. Aarauer Studentenkonferenz, 1926*, 39–64. Berlin: Fürche-Verlag, 1926.
5. *Die Absolutheit Jesu*. 2d ed. Stimmen aus der deutschen christlichen Studentenbewegung, no. 47. Berlin: Fürche-Verlag, 1926.
6. *Die Absolutheit Jesu*. 2d ed.? Stimmen aus der deutschen christlichen Studentenbewegung, no. 47. Berlin: Fürche-Verlag, 1932.
7. *Die Absolutheit Jesu*. 3d ed.? Berlin: Fürche-Verlag, 1934.
8. "Das Aergernis der Nichteinheit der Kirche." *Der Grundriss* 7 (1945).
9. "Das Aergernis der Oxford-Gruppenbewegung." *Neue Zürcher Zeitung* (November 1935).
10. "Der Alkoholismus und unsere Verantwortlichkeit." *Neue Zürcher Zeitung* (April 1946).
11. "Die Alternative zum Nihilismus der Gegenwart." *Reformatio* 1 (1952).
12. "Die andere Aufgabe der Theologie." *Zwischen den Zeiten* 7 (1929): 255–76.
13. "Von der Angst. Vortrag gehalten am 24. Aug. 1953 auf der zweiten CVJM-Europa-Konferenz in Kassel." *Pastoral Blätter* 93 (1953).
14. "And Should Communism Be Victorious?" *Christian Economics* 13 (September 5, 1961): 2–3.

15. "Answer to the Question: Can You Prove God to Me?" *World Communique* 7 (1948).
16. "Antwort an Herrn Heinr. Marti. (Betrifft die Oxfordgruppenbewegung)." *Neue Wege* 30 (1936).
17. "Die Antwort eines Schweizer Theologen auf die Frage: Was geht uns Amerika an?" *Kontakt. Taschenzeitschrift der Jungen* 2 (1959).
18. "Der Apostel Paulus." *Christ und Welt* 3 (1950). This is an excerpt only.
19. "Der Apostel Paulus." In *Paulus-Hellas-Oikumene. Ein Oekumenisches Symposium*, 3–9. Athens: Christian Student Union of Greece, 1951.
20. "Der Apostel Paulus." *Schweizer Monatshefte* 30 (1950).
21. "Der Apostel Paulus." *Universitas* 6 (1951)
22. "Arbeit, Lohn, und Eigentum." *Der Grundriss* 4 (1942).
23. "Auch eine Geheimschtift. Biblische Betrachtung." In *Gemeindeblatt für die ref. Kirchgemeinden des Kantons Glarus* 11 (1924).
24. "Auf der Suche nach einem internationalen Ethos." *Reformatio* 6 (1957).
25. "Die Aufgabe der Christen an der Welt. Ansprache in der St. Annakapelle an der Allianzwoche 1926." *Monatsblatt der Evang. Gesellschaft des Kantons Zürich* 9 (1926).
26. "Aus dem weniger bekannten Amerika." *Kirchenblatt für die reformierte Schweiz*. 35 (1920).
27. "Aus der Tiefe. Predigt in der Universitätskirche Marburg am 15. Sept. 1929." *Zwischen den Zeiten* 8 (1930).
28. "Autobiographische Skizze." *Reformatio* 12 (December, 1963): 631–46.
29. "Banalität oder Irrlehre. Zum Problem der Anthropologie und des Anknüpfungspunktes." *Kirchenblatt für die reformierte Schweiz*. 96 (1940).
30. *Bausteine geistigen Lebens; Ausschnitte aus den Werken von Emil Brunner zusammengestellt von Ernst Hermann Müller-Schürch*. Edited by Ernst Hermann Müller-Schürch. Zurich: Zwingli-Verlag, 1939.
31. "Bach, der Spielman Gottes. Predigt, geh. am Internat. Bach-Fest 1946 in Schaffhausen." *Musik un Gottesdienst: Zeitschrift für evangelische Kirchenmusik*. 1 (1946).
32. "Die bedeutung der missionarischen Erfahrun für die Theologie." In *Die deutsche evangelische Heidenmission, Jahrbuch*

1933 der Vereinigten deutschen Missionkonferenzen, 3–11. Hamburg: Selbstverlag der Missionskonferenzen, 1933.
33. "Die bedeutung der systematischen Theologie für die Gemeinde." *Der Kirchenfreund* 75 (1940).
34. *Die Bedeutung des Abendmahls*. Bern: Gotthelf-Verlag, 1933.
35. "Die Bedeutung des Alten Testaments für unsern Glaube." *Zwischen den Zeiten* 8 (1930): 30–48.
36. "Die Bedeutung des Theologischen Wörtherbuches zum Neuen Testament für die Theologie." In *Theologisches Wörterbuch z. N.T.*, Vol. 4, ?13. Stuttgart: ?Kohlhammer, August, 1940.
37. "Die bedrohung des Menschen und der lebendige Gott." *Universitas* 13 (1958). Also published under the title "Das Nichts oder Gott."
38. "Begegnung mit Kierkegaard." *Der Lesezirkel* 17 (1930).
39. "Die Beichte und die protestantische Kirche der Gegenwart." *Der Kirchenfreund* 70 (1936).
40. "Beitrag zu: Ergebnis einer höchst aktuellen Rundfrage." *Das Schweizerische Rote Kreuz* 67 (1958).
41. "Beitrag zur Umfrage: Welches war mein nachhaltigstes Weihnachtserlebnis?" *Reformierte Schweiz* 16 (1959)
42. "Beitrag zur Umfrage: Wir und die farbigen Völker." *Die Weltwoche* 27 (October 1959).
43. "Beitrag zur Umfrage: Wie war Ihre erste Reaktion auf das Weltuntergangs-Geschwätz?" *Sie und Er* 36 (July 1960).
44. "Bettag 1942." *Neue Zürcher Zeitung* (September 1942).
45. "Bettag 1947." *Neue Zürcher Zeitung* (September 1947).
46. "Von der Bibel dem Worte Gottes." *Kirchenbote für den Kanton Zürich* 37 (1951).
47. "Biblische Psychologie als Grundlage der Erziehung." *Die evangelische Pädagogik* 5 (1936): 121–36.
48. "Bolschewismus und Christentum." *Neue Schweizer Rundschau* 7 (1940).
49. "Die Botschaft Sören Kierkegaards. Rede vor dem Lesezirkel hottingen Zürich." 23 *Neue Schweizer Rundschau* (1930).
50. "Das Brot des Abendmahles und das tägliche Brot." In *Zwinglikalender 1946*. Basel: Reinhardt, 1946.
51. "Cela va de soi . . ." In *Donnez-nous des Messiers!*, 8–10. n.p.: Agence de la Croix Bleue: 1952.
52. "Christentum und Bildung." *Neue Schweizer Rundschau* 8 (1941).
53. *Christentum und Bildung*. Zurich: Fretz & Wasmuth, 1941.

54. "Das Christentum und die Mächte der Zeit. Einleitung zu einem Vorlesungs zyklus an der Universität Zürich." *Neue Schweizer Rundschau* 7 (1939).
55. *Christentum und Kultur*, Edited by Rudolf Wehrli. Zurich: Theologischer Verlag, 1979.
56. *The Christian Doctrine of Creation and Redemption*. Dogmatics II. Translated by Olive Wyon. Lutterworth Library, no. 39. London: Lutterworth Press, 1952. The second volume of Brunner's systematic theology sets out in detail a discussion of the *Imago Dei*, in which Brunner distinguishes between the formal and material aspects of the image.
57. *The Christian Doctrine of Creation and Redemption*. Dogmatics II. Translated by Olive Wyon. ?Lutterworth Library, no. 39. London: Lutterworth Press, 1952; reprint, London: Lutterworth Press, 1954.
58. *The Christian Doctrine of Creation and Redemption*. Dogmatics II. Translated by Olive Wyon. Philadelphia: Westminister Press, 1952.
59. *The Christian Doctrine of Creation and Redemption*. Dogmatics II. Translated by Olive Wyon. Philadelphia: Westminister Press, ?1953.
60. *The Christian Doctrine of God*. Dogmatics I. Translated by Olive Wyon. Lutterworth Library, no. 35. London: Lutterworth Press, 1949. Corrects certain errors in the German text.
61. *The Christian Doctrine of God*. Dogmatics I. Translated by Olive Wyon. Philadelphia: Westminster Press, 1950.
62. *The Christian Doctrine of God*. Dogmatics I. Translated by Olive Wyon. London: Lutterworth Press, 1955.
63. *The Christian Doctrine of God*. Dogmatics I. Translated by Olive Wyon. Philadelphia: Westminster Press, 1950; reprint, Philadelphia: Westminster Press, 1980.
64. *The Christian Doctrine of the Church, Faith and the Consummation*. Dogmatics III. Translated by David Cairns in collaboration with T. H. L. Parker. Philadelphia: Westminster Press, 1960. See notes under *Die Christliche lehre von der Kirche, vom Glauben und von der Vollendung*.
65. *The Christian Doctrine of the Church, Faith and the Consummation*. Dogmatics III. Translated by David Cairns in collaboration with T. H. L. Parker. Philadelphia: Westminster Press, 1960; reprint, Philadelphia: Westminster Press, 1962.
66. *The Christian Doctrine of the Church, Faith and the Consum-*

mation. Dogmatics III. Translated by David Cairns in collaboration with T. H. L. Parker. Lutterworth Library. London: Lutterworth Press, 1962.
67. *The Christian Doctrine of the Church, Faith and the Consummation. Dogmatics III.* Translated by David Cairns in collaboration with T. H. L. Parker. Philadelphia: Westminster Press, 1960; reprint, Philadelphia: Westminster Press, ?1978
68. "The Christian Message to Post War Youth." In *Preparatory Documents. World's Committee of Y.M.C.A.'s.* Geneva: n.p., 1947.
69. "The Christian Idea of God." *World Communique* 7 (1948).
70. "The Christian Idea of God." *Ceylon Men* 5 (February, 1949).
71. "The Christian University and its Importance for Japan." In *Food for All People, No. 1.* Mitaka-Tokyo: Institute of Education Research and Service, International Christian University, 1954.
72. "Christianisme et démocratie." *La vie protestante* 8 (1945).
73. *Christianity and Civilisation.* 2 vols. in 1. New York: Charles Scribner's Sons, 1955. In part one, Brunner deals with the foundational issues, trying to set out a Christian doctrine or philosophy of the foundations of civilization. In the second part, aptly entitled "specific problems," he devotes separately entitled chapters to each of the following areas: technics, science, tradition and renewal, education, work, art, wealth, social custom (*Sitte*) and law, and power. A concluding chapter and epilog round out the second volume, and return to foundational issues raised in the first.
74. *Christianity and Civilisation (Gifford Lectures, 1947–48).* 2 vols. in 1. New York: AMS Press, 1981.
75. *Christianity and Civilisation, First Part: Foundations.* New York: Charles Scribner's Sons, 1948.
76. *Christianity and Civilisation. First Part: Foundations. (Gifford Lectures, delivered at the University of St. Andrews, 1947).* London: John Nisbet & Co., 1948.
77. *Christianity and Civilisation (Gifford Lectures, 1947–1948): Part 1—Foundations.* London: John Nisbet & Co., 1948–49.
78. *Christianity and Civilisation (Gifford Lectures, 1947–1948): Part 2: Specific Problems.* London: John Nisbet & Co., 1948–49.
79. *Christianity and Civilisation (Gifford Lectures, 1947–1948): Part I—Foundations.* London: John Nisbet & Co., ?1955.

80. *Christianity and Civilisation (Gifford Lectures, 1947–1948): Part II—Specific Problems.* London: John Nisbet & Co., ?1955.
81. *Christianity and Civilisation, Second Part: Specific Problems.* New York: Charles Scribner's Sons, 1949.
82. *Christianity and Culture. First Takeshi Saito Lecture, delivered on 19 Jan. 1955 at Tokyo Joshi Daigaku.* Tokyo: The Academic Society of Tokyo Women's Christian College, 1955.
83. *Christianity in the Age of Crisis. Four Lectures at YWCA Tokyo.* Tokyo: YWCA, 1957. Original may have been in Japanese. The four lectures were: 1. What is the Meaning of Life? 2. On Human Happiness 3. The Christian Idea of Love and the Modern World 4. The Time of Crisis and the Practice of Faith.
84. *Christianity in the World Today. Four Lectures.* Tokyo: Y.M.C.A., 1949. Japanese Text of 110 pages. The four lectures were: 1. Spiritual Foundations of Democracy 2. Christianity and the Crisis of Culture 3. Christianity and the Middle Road 4. The Task of the Church Today.
85. "The Christian Understanding of Man." In *The Christian Understanding of Man.* Church, Community and State Series, no. 2., ed.? T. E. Jessop, 139–78. London: G. Allen & Unwin Ltd., 1938. Derived from the World Conference on Church, Community and State, Oxford, 1937.
86. "The Christian Understanding of Man." In *The Christian Understanding of Man: The Official Oxford Conference Books, Vol. II,* ed.? T. E. Jessop, ?139–78. Chicago: Willet, Clark & Company, 1938. Derived from the World Conference on Church, Community and State, Oxford, 1937.
87. "The Christian Understanding of Time." *Scottish Journal of Theology* 4 (March 1951): 1–12.
88. "Der Christ im Staat." *Neue Schweizer Rundschau* ?2 (1934).
89. "Das christliche Erbe." In *Beiträge zu: Eidg. Rechenschaft und Verpflichtung.* n.p.: n.p., 1941.
90. "Das christliche Erbe." *Neue Zürcher Zeitung* (April 1941).
91. "Der christliche Glaube als Grundlage der Erziehung." In *Schweiz evang. Schulblatt* 65 (1930).
92. "Die christliche Nicht-Kirche-Bewegung in Japan. Gottlob Schrenk, dem Mann der Mission, zum 80. Geburtstag." *Evang. Theologie* 19 (1959).
93. *Christlicher Existenzialismus. Vortrag, gehalten vor der Studen-*

tenschaft der Universität Zürich. Kirchliche Zeitfragen, no. 39. Zurich: Zwingli-Verlag, 1956.
94. "Christlicher Existenzialismus. Vortrag, gehalten vor der Studentenschaft der Universität Zürich." *Neue Zürcher Zeitung* (March 1956).
95. "Christlicher Glaube nach reformierter Lehre." In *Der Protestantismus der Gegenwart: Unter mitwirkung Führender Persönlichkeiten des Kirchlichen und Theologisch-Wissenschaftlichen Lebens,* ed. G. Schenkel, 235–69. Stuttgart: Verlag Friedr. Bohnenberger, 1926.
96. "Christlicher Glaube und Philosophie der Existenz." In *Philosophie und christliche Existenz: Festschrift für Heinrich Barth zum 70. Geburtstag,* ed. Gerhard Hüber, 119–30. Basel: Verlag Helbling und Lichtenhahn, 1960.
97. *Die Christliche lehre von der Kirche, vom Glauben und von der Vollendung.* Dogmatik III. Zurich: Zwingli-Verlag, 1960. The third volume of Brunner's systematic theology was long delayed due to ill health and involvement in other projects. The third volume is not of the same standard of the first two. The impression is that of an author trying in frantic haste to tie up loose ends.
98. *Die Christliche lehre von Gott.* Dogmatik I. Zurich: Zwingli-Verlag, 1946. First edition of this work.
99. *Die Christliche lehre von Gott.* 3d ed.? Dogmatik I. Zurich: Zwingli-Verlag, 1960.
100. *Die Christliche lehre von Schöpfung und Erlösung.* Dogmatik II. Zurich: Zwingli-Verlag, 1950. First edition of this work.
101. *Die Christliche lehre von Schöpfung und Erlösung.* 2d ed.? Dogmatik II. Zurich: Zwingli-Verlag, 1960.
102. "Zum christlichen Verständnis des Staates." *Neue Zürcher Zeitung* (June 1944).
103. *Christlicher Existenzialismus.* Kirkliche Zeitfragen, no. 39. Zurich: Zwingli-Verlag, 1956.
104. "Der christliche Staat." In *Geisteserbe der Schweiz,* ed. Eduard Corrodi, 413–25. Erlenbach: Rentsch, 1943.
105. "Der christliche Staat." In *Vom Wesen der Eidgenossenschaft. Ansprache, geh. an der akad. Feier: 650 Jahre Eidgenossenschaft, am 21. Juni 1941 in der Aula der Universität Zürich,* 21–7. Zurich: Orell Fussli, 1941.
106. "Der christliche Staatsmann." In *Festgabe für Max Hüber zum 60. Geburtstag,* 240–49. Zurich: Berichthaus, 1934.

107. "Das christliche Zeugnis für die Ordnung der Gesellschaft und des nationalen Lebens. Vortrag, gehalten in Amsterdam anl. der Weltkirchenkonferenz." In *Amsterdamer Dokumente. 1. Beiheft zur Halbmonatsschrift 'Evangelische Welt'*, 234–43. ?: ?Bethel, 1948.
108. "Christoph Blumhardt." *Neue Zürcher Zeitung* (June 1938).
109. "Zur Christologischen Begründung des Staates." *Kirchenblatt für die reformierte Schweiz.* 99 (January 7–February 4, 1943): 2–5, 18–23, 34–36.
110. "Christ, The Hope of the World." *World Christian Education* (?September, 1954).
111. "Christus am Kreuz, unser Heil." In *Unser Bekenntnis zu Jesus Christus; 4 Vorträge im Fraumünster*, 31–52. Zurich: Zwingli-Verlag, 1938.
112. *Die Christusbotschaft in Kampf mit den Religionen.* Basler Missionsstudien Neue Folge, no. 8. Stuttgart: Evang. Missionsverlag, 1931. Important work for understanding Brunner's view of non-Christian religions, and their relationship to Christianity.
113. *Die Christusbotschaft in Kampf mit den Religionen.* Stuttgart: Evang. Missionsverlag, 1931.
114. "Die Christusbotschaft und der Staat." *Der Grundriss* 2 (February 1940).
115. *Die Christusbotschaft und der Staat.* Zurich: Zwingli-Verlag, 1940.
116. "Christus ist die Antwort." In *Zwinglikalender 1954.* Basel: Reinhardt, 1954.
117. *The Church and the Oxford Group.* Translated by David Cairns. London: Hodder and Stoughton, 1937. This is a translation of *Die Kirchen, die Gruppenbewegung und die Kirche Jesus Christi.*
118. "The Church as a Gift and a Task. Lecture delivered on April 1, 1954, at the Kyodan-related Missionary Conference at Yumoto" *Japan Christian Quarterly* 20 (July 1954): 183–193.
119. "The Church Between East and West. An Address Delivered to the Assembly of the Congregational Union of England and Wales, May, 1949." *The Congregational Quarterly* 27 (July 1949): 204–17.
120. *The Church in the New Social Order: An Address Delivered to the National Congress of the Free Church, Federal Council,*

Cardiff, on 26th March, 1952. London: SCM Press Ltd., 1952.
121. *Communism, Capitalism and Christianity.* Translated by Norman P. Goldhawk. London: Lutterworth Press, 1949.
122. *Communism, Capitalism and Christianity.* Translated by Norman P. Goldhawk. Sydney: Agnus and Robertson, 1949.
123. "Continental European Theology." Translated by Olive Dutche-Doggett. In *The Church Through Half a Century: Essays in Honor of William Adams Brown*, eds. Samuel McCrea Cavert and Henry Pitney van Dusen. 133–44. New York: Charles Scribner's Sons, 1936.
124. "The Crisis of Psychology." *The Student World* 23 (1930).
125. "Critic or Apologist of Civilization?" *Religion in Life* 20 (Summer 1951): 323–28.
126. "Da dürfen wir nicht schweigen. Ansprache, geh. an der Sympathiekundgebung der Studentenschaft der Zürcher Hochschulen für den Kampf der norwegischen Akademiker." *Neue Zürcher Zeitung* (December 1943).
127. "The Decline of the Occident." *The World Tomorrow* (November 1921). This is a review of Spengler's *Untergang des Abendlandes.*
128. "Denken und Erleben." In *Vorträge an der Asrauer Studentenkonferenz, 1919*, 5–34. Basel: Kober, 1919.
129. *Die denkwürdige Geschichte der Mayflower-Pilgerväter.* Basel: Reinhardt, 1920.
130. "Deutschlands Not." *Neue Zürcher Zeitung* (May, 1947). Translated into English under the titles "Germany's Distress" and "De-Nazification to Re-Nazification."
131. *The Divine-Human Encounter.* Translated by Amandus W. Loos. Philadelphia: Westminster Press, 1943. See notes under *Truth as Encounter.*
132. *The Divine-Human Encounter.* Translated by Amandus W. Loos. Toronto: Ambassador Books, Ltd., 1943.
133. *The Divine-Human Encounter.* Translated by Amandus W. Loos. Philadelphia: Westminster Press, 1943; reprint, Philadelphia: Westminster Press, 1944.
134. *The Divine-Human Encounter.* Translated by Amandus W. Loos. London: Student Christian Movement Press Ltd., 1944.
135. *The Divine-Human Encounter.* Translated by Amandus W. Loos. Westport, Conn.: Greenwood Press, 1980.
136. *The Divine Imperative: A Study in Christian Ethics.* Trans-

lated by Olive Wyon. Lutterworth Library Series, no. 7. London: Lutterworth Press, 1937.
137. *The Divine Imperative: A Study in Christian Ethics.* 2d ed.? Translated by Olive Wyon. New York: Macmillan Company, 1937.
138. *The Divine Imperative: A Study in Christian Ethics.* Translated by Olive Wyon. New York: Macmillan Company, 1942.
139. *The Divine Imperative: A Study in Christian Ethics.* Translated by Olive Wyon. London: Lutterworth Press, 1937; reprint, London: Lutterworth Press, 1949.
140. *The Divine Imperative: A Study in Christian Ethics.* Translated by Olive Wyon. Philadelphia: Westminster Press, 1947.
141. *The Divine Imperative: A Study in Christian Ethics.* Translated by Olive Wyon. Lutterworth Library, no. 7. London: Lutterworth Press, 1951.
142. *The Divine Imperative: A Study in Christian Ethics.* Translated by Olive Wyon. Philadelphia: Westminster Press, 1957.
143. *The Divine Imperative: A Study in Christian Ethics.* Translated by Olive Wyon. London: Lutterworth Press, 1937; reprint, London: Lutterworth Press, 1964.
144. "La Doctrine Chretienne du Dieu Createur. Conférence prononcée le 29 Mai, 1950 devant la Société des pastors Vaudois." Translated from the German by Etienne Trocmé. *Revue d'histoire et de Philosophie Religieuses* 34 (?October/December 1954): 325–41.
145. *Dogmatics.* 2 vols. Translated by Olive Wyon. Lutterworth Library, nos. 35, 39. London: Lutterworth Press, 1957. Library of Congress Catalog lists this as "2nd Printing" but gives no details regarding a first printing.
146. *Dogmatics: The Christian Doctrine of Creation and Redemption.* Translated by Olive Wyon. Lutterworth Library. London: Lutterworth Press, 1952; reprint, London: Lutterworth Press, 1964.
147. *Dogmatics: The Christian Doctrine of God.* Translated by Olive Wyon. Lutterworth Library. London: Lutterworth Press, 1949; reprint, London: Lutterworth Press, 1964.
148. *Dogmatics: The Christian Doctrine of the Church, Faith and the Consummation.* Translated by Olive Wyon. Lutterworth Library. London: Lutterworth Press, 1962; reprint, London: Lutterworth Press, 1964.

149. *Dogmatik: Die Christliche lehre von der Kirche, vom Glauben and von der Vollendung.* Zurich: Zwingli-Verlag, 1960.
150. *Dogmatik: Die Christliche lehre von Gott.* 3d? ed. Zurich: Zwingli-Verlag, 1960.
151. *Dogmatik: Die Christliche lehre von Schöpfung und Erlösung.* 2d ed.? Zurich: Zwingli-Verlag, 1960.
152. "Vom Dollar, von Christentum und einigem andern in Amerika." In *Zwinglikalendar, 1924.* Basel: Reinhardt: 1924.
153. "Do you see any hopeful basis of Protestant-Roman Catholic Church Unity? 25 Scholars' Views." *Christianity Today* 5 (October 10, 1960): 29–32, 34, 38.
154. *Drei Predigten vom ewigen Leben.* Zurich: Zwingli-Verlag, 1942.
155. "Duplik (Betrifft die Auseinandersetzung mit L. Köhler)." 41 *Kirchenblatt für die reformierte Schweiz* (1926).
156. "Easter Certainty [excerpt from sermon]." *Theology Today* 18 (April 1961): 14, 15.
157. "Ecclesia and Evangelism: A Message to the General Assembly of the United Church of Christ in Japan, Oct. 27, 1954." *Japan Christian Quarterly* 21 (April 1955): 154–59.
158. *Les églises, les groupes et l'église de Jésus-Christ.* Translated by A. R. T. Geneva: Editions Labor, 1937.
159. "Das Einmalige und der Existenz-charakter." *Blatter für deutsche Philosophie* 3 (1929).
160. "Das Einmalige und die Geschichte." In *Hortulus Amicorum. Fritz Ernst zum 60. Geburtstag*, 45–49. Zurich: Fretz & Wasmuth, 1949.
161. *Eiserne Ration.* Tornister Bibliothek, no. 1. Erlenbach: Eugen Rentsch, 1939.
162. *Die Ekklesia des Neuen Testamentes und die CVJM.* Merkblätter für CVJM Arbeit. Bern: Bundeszentrale der CVJM der Deutschsprachigen Schweiz, 1956.
163. "Das Elend der Theologie. Ein Nachwort zum Zurcher Ferienkurs, zugleich ein Vorwort." *Kirchenblatt für die reformierte Schweiz.* 35 (1920).
164. "Emil Brunner on His Faith and Work. A Television Interview with Vernon Sproxton." *The Listener and B.B.C. Television Review* 65 (February, 1961): 307–8.
165. *Emil Brunner on Love & Marriage: Selections from the Divine Imperative.* Edited by Vernon Sproxton. London: Fontana, 1970.

166. "Zu Epprechts Kritik, über *Die Mystik und das Wort.*" *Kirchenblatt für die reformierte Schweiz.* 85 (1929).
167. "Die Erde drecht sich. Eine Erwiderung. (Betrifft einen Aufsatz von Ludwig Köhler über den Sündenfall) *Kirchenblatt für die reformierte Schweiz.* 41 (1926).
168. "Erfahrungen im Fernen Osten." In *Gott füllt leere Hände. Geistliche Woche für Südwestdeutschland. der Evang. Akademie Mannheim vom 15. April–22. April 1956.* Mannheim: Evang. Akademie, 1956.
169. "Der Erfüller. Predigt, geh. in Basel am 25. Mai 1930." *Zwischen den Zeiten* 8 (1930).
170. *Erhalt' uns, Herr, bei deinem Wort! Evangelische Andachten für jeden Tag.* Berlin: Fürche-Verlag, 1931.
171. "Zur Erinnerung an Max Huber." In *Zwinglikalender 1961.* Basel: Reinhardt, 1961.
172. "Erklärungen zum Fall Gerstenmaier." *Kirchenblatt für die reformierte Schweiz.* 101 (1945).
173. *Erlebnis, Erkenntnis und Glaube.* Zurich: Zwingli-Verlag, 1938.
174. *Erlebnis, Erkenntnis und Glaube.* Tubingen: Verlag J. C. B. Mohr (Paul Siebeck), 1921.
175. *Erlebnis, Erkenntnis und Glaube.* 2d. ed. rev. Tübingen: Verlag J. C. B. Mohr (Paul Siebeck), 1923.
176. *Erlebnis, Erkenntnis und Glaube.* 3d ed. rev. Tübingen: Verlag J. C. B. Mohr (Paul Siebeck), 1923.
177. *Erlebnis, Erkenntnis und Glaube.* Tübingen: Verlag J. C. B. Mohr (Paul Siebeck), 1933.
178. *Um die Erneuerung der Kirche. Ein Wort an alle, die sie lieb haben.* Bern: Gotthelf-Verlag, 1934. Also published as *Die Kirche als Frage und Aufgabe der Gegenwart.*
179. *Um die Erneuerung der kirche. Ein Wort an alle, die sie lieb haben.* Bern: Gotthelf-Verlag, 1934.
180. "Die Ernte ist gross, aber wenige sind der Arbeiter. Missionspredigt." In *Zu Einem Zeugnis über alle Völker*, 5–14. Stuttgart: Evang. Missions-Verlag, 1937.
181. "Eros und Gewissen bei Gottfried Keller." In *Neujahrsblatt auf das Jahr 1965; zum Besten des Waisenhauses*, ed. Der Gelehrten Gesellschaft, ?128. Zurich: n.p., ?1965.
182. *Eros und Gewissen bei Gottfried Keller.* Zurich: Kommissionsverlag Beer, 1965.

183. "Eros und Liebe: ein Vortrag." *Neue Schweizer Rundschau* 5 (September 1933).
184. *Eros und Liebe: Vom Sinn und Geheimnis unserer Existenz.* Fürche-Bücherei, no. 32. Berlin: Fürche-Verlag, 1937.
185. *Eros und Liebe: Vom Sinn und Geheimnis unserer Existenz.* Hamburg: Fürche-Verlag, 1952.
186. *Eternal Hope.* Translated by Harold Knight. Philadelphia: Westminster Press, 1954. See notes under German title *Das Ewige als Zukunft und Gegenwart.*
187. *Eternal Hope.* Translated by Harold Knight. London: Lutterworth Press, 1954.
188. *Eternal Hope.* Translated by Harold Knight. Philadelphia: Westminster Press, 1954; reprint, Westport, Conn.: Greenwood Press, 1972.
189. *The Ethical Reality and Function of the Church.* Geneva: Study Divisions of the Ecumenical Council for Life and Work, 1942.
190. "Die ethische Bedeutung des christlichen Dogmas. IV. Der Glaube an Gott, den Schöpfer. 2. Teil. Die Schöpfungsordnungen und der Bolschewismus." *Der Grundriss* 1 (1939).
191. "Die ethische Bedeutung des christlichen Dogmas. III. Ich glaube an Gott, den Schöpfer." *Der Grundriss* 1 (1939).
192. "Die ethische Bedeutung des christlichen Dogmas. II. Das grosse Misverständnis des Glaubens." *Der Grundriss* 1 (1939).
193. "Die ethische Bedeutung des christlichen Dogmas. I. Lehre und Leben." *Der Grundriss* 1 (1939).
194. "Die ethische Bedeutung des christlichen Dogmas. V. Die Menschwerdung des Gottessohnes." *Der Grundriss* 2 (1940).
195. "Die ethische Bedeutung des christlichen Dogmas VII. Die Rechtfertigung des Sünders." *Der Grundriss* 2 (1940).
196. "Die ethische Bedeutung des christlichen Dogmas. VI. Die versöhnung." *Der Grundris* 2 (1940).
197. "Etwas von Konfirmandenunterricht." *Gemeindeblatt für die ref. Kirchgemeinden des Kantons Glarus* 5 (1918).
198. *Europe and America: A Contribution to Mutual Understanding. (Lecture held at the General Meeting of the Swiss-American Society for Cultural Relations, Bern, 1951).* Translated by Mary Hottinger. Zurich: Swiss-American Society for Cultural Relations, 1952.
199. "Zur evang. Ethik und Wirtschaftsethik." *Kirchenblatt für die reformierte Schweiz.* 85 (1929).

200. *Das Ewige als Zukunft und Gegenwart*. Zurich: Zwingli-Verlag, 1952. Translated into English as *Eternal Hope*. This study of last things resulted from Brunner's grief over the death of his second son in a 1952 railway accident.
201. *Das Ewige als Zukunft und Gegenwart*. Zurich: Zwingli-Verlag, 1952; reprint, Zurich: Zwingli-Verlag,1953.
202. *Das Ewige als Zukunft und Gegenwart*. Siebenstern-Taschenbuch, no. 32. Zurich: Zwingli-Verlag, 1953; reprint, Munich: Siebenstern Taschenbuch Verlag, 1965.
203. *Faith, Hope and Love*. Philadelphia: Westminster Press, 1956. Originally the Earl Lectures, 1955.
204. *Faith, Hope and Love*. Toronto: Ryerson Press, 1956.
205. *Faith, Hope and Love*. London: Lutterworth Press, 1957.
206. "Falscher und wahrer Biblizismus." *Kirchenblatt für die reformierte Schweiz*. 100 (May 4, 1944): 134–37.
207. "Die Familie als Schöpfungsordnung." *Du* 1 (1941).
208. "Familie und reformatorischer Glaube." *Atlantis* 4 (1932): 736–44.
209. "Festen Boden unter den Füssen. Radioansprache." *Volksfreund* (May 1940).
210. "The Foundations of Personalism." *Manhood: Y.M.C.A. National Magazine* 2 (1948).
211. "Zur Frage der Kirchlichen Verantwortung. Zur Diskussion über die Todesstrafe." *Kirchenblatt für die reformierte Schweiz*. 98 (1942).
212. "Zur Frage der theologischen Anthropologie Dialektik und Anthropologie." *Zwischen den Zeiten* 10 (1932): 564–67.
213. "Die Frage nach dem 'Anknüpfungspunkt' als Problem der Theologie." *Zwischen den Zeiten* 10 (1932): 505–32.
214. *Fraumünster Predigten*. Zurich: Zwingli-Verlag, 1953. Translated into English as *The Great Invitation*.
215. *Fraumünsterpredigten*. 2d ed.? Zurich: Zwingli-Verlag, 1955.
216. *Fraumünsterpredigten*. Zurich: Zwingli-Verlag, 1965.
217. "Freiheit als Verantwortlichkeit. Vortrag, gehalten in der Universität Zürich auf Einladung der Kulturwissenschaftl. Abteilung des Schweiz. Instituts für Auslandsforschung." In *Theologia Oecumenica in Honor of William Enkichi Kan*, 15–25. Tokyo: Rikkyo University, 1958.
218. "Freiheit als Verantwortlichkeit. Vortrag, gehalten in der Universität Zürich auf Einladung der Kulturwissenschaftl.

Abteilung des Schweiz. Instituts für Auslandsforschung." *Schweizer Monatshefte* 37 (1957).
219. "Die Freiheit der christlichen Gemeinde in heutigen Staat. Vortrag, geh. am Evang. Seminar Unterstrass." In *Kirche und Schule*, 5–27. Zurich: Zwingli-Verlag, 1944.
220. "Fresh Appraisal: The Cleveland Report on Red China." *Christianity Today* 4 (April 25, 1960): 3–6.
221. "Friede auf Erden." *Neue Zürcher Zeitung* (December 1943).
222. "Friede auf Erden." *Schweizerische Allgem. Volks-Zeitung* 63 (1947).
223. "Friede auf Erden Luk. 2, 14, Weihnachtspredigt 1943." *Der Grundriss* 6 (1944).
224. "Friedenshoffnung, Friedensaufgabe, Friedensillusion." In *Zwinglikalender 1945*. Basel: Reinhardt, 1945.
225. *Das Gebot und die Ordnungen: Entwurf einer protestantisch-theologischen Ethik*. Berlin: Fürche-Verlag, 1932. During the late 1920s and 30s Brunner was preoccupied with the problem of the nature of humanity. He was driven to this study partly because of the rise of totalitarian states in Europe, both fascist and communist. Brunner opposed both ideologies because he considered them to be based on a faulty understanding of what a human being was. The human was to Brunner, first and foremost a person responsible before God. This volume was the first outworking of this study of human nature. It argues that God's first command is the command to love, and all other commands are derived from this.
226. *Das Gebot und die Ordnungen: Entwurf einer protestantisch-theologischen Ethik*. 2d ed.? Berlin: Fürche-Verlag, 1932.
227. *Das Gebot und die Ordnungen: Entwurf einer protestantisch-theologischen Ethik*. Tübingen: Verlag J. C. B. Mohr (Paul Siebeck), 1932.
228. *Das Gebot und die Ordnungen: Entwurf einer protestantisch-theologischen Ethik*. 2d ed.? Tübingen: Verlag J. C. B. Mohr (Paul Siebeck), 1933.
229. *Das Gebot und die Ordnungen: Entwurf einer protestantisch-theologischen Ethik*. 3d ed.? Zurich: Zwingli-Verlag, 1939.
230. *Das Gebot und die Ordnungen: Entwurf einer protestantisch-theologischen Ethik*. 4th ed.? Zurich: Zwingli-Verlag, 1939.
231. *Das Gebot und die Ordnungen: Entwurf einer protestantisch-theologischen Ethik*. New York: Kommission des ökumenischen Rates der Kirchen, ?1945.

232. *Das Gebot und die Ordnungen: Entwurf einer protestantisch-theologischen Ethik.* Zurich: Theologischer Verlag, 1978.
233. "Gehort Politik auf die Kanzel?" *Der Grundriss* 4 (1942).
234. *Geistige Hindernisse und Brücken zwischen Amerika und Europa. Vortrag gehalten an der Generalversammlung der Swiss-American Society for Cultural Relations, am 17. November, 1951 in Bern.* n.p.: n.p., ?1952.
235. "Geistige Hindernisse und Brucken zwischen Amerika und Europa. Vortrag gehalten an der Generalversammlung der Swiss-American Society for Cultural Relations, am 17. November, 1951 in Bern." *Neue Schweizer Rundschau* 19 (1951).
236. "Die geistigen Ursachen der Ehekrise. Vortrag am 1. Okt. 1943, geh. am Kongress Pro Familia im Kongresshaus Zurich." In *Kongressbericht "Pro Familia"*, 6–16. Zurich: Zentralsekretariat Pro Juventute, 1943.
237. "Die geistigen Ursachen der Ehekrise. Vortrag am 1. Okt. 1943, geh. am Kongress Pro Familia im Kongresshaus Zürich." In *Kirchenbote für den Kanton Zürich* (February, 1944).
238. "Die geistigen Voraussetzungen eines Neuaufbaus." *Neue Schweizer Rundschau* 13 (1945).
239. "Der Geist und die Triebe in der Geschichte." *Neue Zürcher Zeitung* (June 1926).
240. "Geist und Form in der Demokratie." *Neue Zürcher Zeitung* (July 1944).
241. "Geist (Zum Pfingfest)." *Gemeindeblatt für die ref. Kirchgemeinden des Kantons Glarus* 3 (1916).
242. "Das Geld und der Haushalt Gottes. Ein seltsamer Katechismus." In *Zwinglikalender 1932*. Basel: Reinhardt, 1932.
243. "Gemeinschaft." In *Zwinglikalender 1934*. Basel: Reinhardt, 1934.
244. "Der gerechte Zins." *Der Grundriss* 5 (1943).
245. *Der gerechte Zins.* Zurich: Zwingli-Verlag, 1943.
246. "Gerechtigkeit." *Neue Zürcher Zeitung* (November 1947). This and preceding item form Chapter 18 of Brunner's book *Gerechtigkeit*.
247. *Gerechtigkeit, eine Lehre von den Grundgesetzen der Gesellschafts Ordnung.* Zurich: Zwingli-Verlag, 1943. Translated into English under the title *Justice and the Social Order*, this book follows the usual Brunner pattern. In Part I, foundational issues are considered such as the nature of justice, and

the concept of justice in Scripture. In Part II, the principles set out are applied to specific practical situations including the place of justice in the political sphere, in the family, the economy, and on the international political stage.

248. "Germany's Distress." *Christianity and Crisis* 7 (1947): 3–5.
249. "Geschichte oder Offenbarung? Ein Wort der Entgegnung an Horst Stephan." *Zeitschrift für Theologie und Kirche* 6 (1925).
250. "Gesetz und Offenbarung. Eine theologische Grundlegung." *Theologische Blätter* 4 (1925).
251. "Gewissenloser Journalismus." *Neue Zürcher Zeitung* (September 1943).
252. "Gibt es eine allgemeine neutrale Staatsmoral?" *Neue Zürcher Zeitung* (January 1927).
253. "Gibt es eine religionlose Moral? Vortrag, geh. an der Maiversammlung 1928 der ehemal. Schüler des Seminars Unterstrass, Zürich." *Schweiz evang. Schulblatt* 63 (1928).
254. "Gibt es geistliches Recht?" *Kirchenblatt für die reformierte Schweiz.* 41 (1926).
255. "Glaube und Erziehung." In *Zwinglikalender 1928*. Basel: Reinhardt, 1928.
256. *Glaube und Ethik. Vortrag, geh. in der Kunstgesellschaft Thun*. Thun: Krebser & Co., 1945.
257. "Glaube und Forschung. Festrede des Rektors, geh. an der 110. Stiftungsfeier der Universität Zürich, am 29. April 1943." In *Jahresbericht 1942/43*, ?ed. Georges Méautis, 3–20. Zurich: Orell Fussli, 1943.
258. "Glaube und Leben. Zwei Vorträge aus der Vorlesung an der Volkschochschule Zürich, Wintersem. 1929/30." *Der Kirchenfreund* 64 (1930).
259. "Gnade Gottes: V. Dogmatisch." In *Religion in Geschichte und Gegenwart. Handwörterbuch für Theologie und Religionswissenschaft*, ed. W. Joest, 1261–68. 2d ed. Tübingen: J. C. B. Mohr, 1928.
260. "Gnade Gottes: V. Dogmatisch." In *Religion in Geschichte und Gegenwart. Handwörterbuch für Theologie und Religionswissenschaft*, ed. Wilfred Warbeck. 3d ed. Tübingen: J. C. B. Mohr (Paul Siebeck), 1958.
261. *God and Man: Four Essays on the Nature of Personality*. Translated by David Cairns. London: SCM Press Ltd., 1936.
262. *God and Man: Four Essays on the Nature of Personality*. Translated by David Cairns. New York: Macmillan, 1936.

263. "The Gospel and Modern India. Speech at the Convocation of Sarampore College, held on Saturday, Jan. 21, 1950." *Serampore College Magazine and the Students' Chronicle* 7 (1950)
264. "Der Gott, der Wunder tut." In *Zwinglikalender 1950*. Basel: Reinhardt, 1950.
265. "Göttliche und menschliche Weisheit." *Der Kirchenfreund* ?81 (1947).
266. "Göttliche und menschliche Weisheit." *Evangelisch-soziale Warte* (1947).
267. *Gott und das Brot: Predigt von Emil Brunner über Mat. 4, 1–4*. Bern: Gotthelf-Verlag, 1930.
268. *Gott und Mensch: Vier Untersuchungen über das personhafte Sein*. Tübingen: Verlag J. C. B. Mohr (Paul Siebeck), 1930.
269. *Gott und Mensch: Vier Untersuchungen über das personhafte Sein*. Zurich: Zwingli-Verlag, 1938.
270. *Gott und Mensch: Predigt über Gal. 4, 4–7*. Zurich: Zwingli-Verlag, 1940.
271. *Gott und sein Rebell. Eine theologische Anthropologie*. Edited by Ursula Berger-Gebhardt. Rowohlts deutsche Enzyclopädie Series. Hamburg: Rohwohlt, 1958. Apparently a student edition of *Der Mensch in Widerspruch*.
272. *Gott ward Mensch: Predigt über Gal. 4, 4–7*. Zurich: Zwingli-Verlag, 1940.
273. *The Great Invitation and other Sermons*. Translated by Harold Knight. Philadelphia: Westminster Press, 1955. Originally published in German as *Fraümunster Predigten*.
274. *The Great Invitation: Zurich Sermons of Emil Brunner*. Translated by Harold Knight. London: Lutterworth Press, 1955.
275. "A Great Time for Preaching." *The Christian Century* 68 (1951).
276. *Die Grenzen der Humanität. Habilitationsvorlesung an der Universität Zürich*. Sammlung gemeinverständlicher Vorträge und Schriften aus dem Gebeite der Theologie und Religionsgeschichte Series, no. 102. Tübingen: J. C. B. Mohr, 1922.
277. "Grisebachs Angriff auf die Theologie." *Zwischen den Zeiten* 6 (1928): 219–232.
278. *Das grosse Wunder. Predigt, geh. in St. Gallen am 10 Febr. 1934*. St. Gallen: Buchhdlg. der Evang. Gesellschaft, 1934.

279. "Grundlagen christlicher Wirtschaftsordnung." *Schweizerischen Arbeitgeber-Zeitung* 14 (April 2, 1942).
280. "Grundlagen christlicher Wirtschaftsordnung." *Schweizerischen Arbeitgeber-Zeitung* 15 (April 10, 1942).
281. "Grundlagen christlicher Wirtschaftsordnung." *Schweizerischen Arbeitgeber-Zeitung* 16 (April 17, 1942).
282. *Grundlagen christlicher Wirtschaftsordnung.* Zurich: E. Ruegg, 1942.
283. *Die Grundlagen nationaler Erziehung. Referat vor der Neuen Helvetischen Gesellschaft in Aarau, 12.* April 1942. Brugg: Effingerhof, 1943.
284. "Die Grundlagen nationaler Erziehung. Referat vor der Neuen Helvetischen Gesellschaft in Aarau, 12. April 1942." In *Jahrsbuch Die Schweiz 1943*, 9.21. Brugg: Effongerhof, 1943.
285. *Das grundproblem der ethik.* Zurich: Rascher & cie., 1931.
286. "Das Grundproblem der Philosophie bei Kant und Kierkegaard. Vortrag vor der Kantgesellschaft in Utrecht, Dez. 1923." In *Zwischen den Zeiten* 2 (1924): 31–46.
287. "Grundsätzliche Erwägungen. Bericht der theologischen Subkommission der Kommission zur Prüfung der Beziehungen zwischen Kirche und Staat, erstattet zu Händen der Gesamtkommission." In *Zürcher Kirchengesetz und christliche Kirche*, 10–33. Zurich: Kirchenrat d. Kts. Zürich, 1939.
288. "Grundsätzliches zum Kapitel Die jungen Theologen." *Kirchenblatt für die reformierte Schweiz.* 31 (1916).
289. "Von guten und vom schlechten Predigten." In *Zwinglikalender 1925.* Basel: Reinhardt, 1925.
290. "Das Haus Gottes. Andact anl. der Pfarrkonferenz am. 9. April 1931." *Kirchenblatt für die reformierte Schweiz.* 87 (1931).
291. "Der heilige Name. Predigt, geh. am 18. Nov. 1928 in der Kirche Oberstrass in Zürich." *Zwischen den Zeiten* 7 (1929): 1–9.
292. "Heilige Ordnung." *Neue Zürcher Zeitung* (December 1941).
293. "Der heilige Wille Gottes." In *Das christliche Leben im Lichte der zehn Gebote.* Zurich: Gotthelf-Verlag, 1942.
294. *Das helle Herz. Weihnachtspredigt 1942.* Zurich: Zwingli-Verlag, 1942.
295. "Herr, lehre uns beten: Das Unservater." In *Zwinglikalender 1938.* Basel: Reinhardt, 1938.

296. "Hochschule und Gymnasium." In *Jahrbuch des Vereins Schweiz. Gymnasiallehrer, Jahrg. 1932*, 40–44. ?Aarau: ?Sauerlander, 1933.
297. "The Hope for Japan. Dr. Brunner's Farewell Address." *The ICU News, Special Issue on Dr. Brunner* (1955)
298. "How Can We Believe in the Myths of Christianity?" *World Communique* 7 (1948).
299. "How Can We Believe in the Myths of Christianity?" *Ceylon Men* 5 (April 1949).
300. "Toward a Missionary Theology: How My Mind Has Changed in the Last Decade." *The Christian Century* 66 (July 6, 1949): 816–18.
301. *I Believe in the Living God: Sermons on the Apostles' Creed.* Translated and edited by John Holden. Philadelphia: Westminster Press, 1959.
302. *I Believe in the Living God: Sermons on the Apostles' Creed.* Translated and edited by John Holden. Toronto: Ryerson Press, 1961.
303. *I Believe in the Living God: Sermons on the Apostles' Creed.* Translated and edited by John Holden. London: Lutterworth Press, 1961.
304. *I Believe in the Living God: Sermons on the Apostles' Creed.* Translated and edited by John Holden. Philadelphia: Westminster Press, 1961.
305. *Ich glaube an den lebendigen Gott: Predigten über das altchristliche Glaubensbekenntnis.* Zurich: Zwingli-Verlag, 1940.
306. *Ich glaube an den lebendigen Gott: Predigten über das altchristliche Glaubensbekenntnis.* 2d ed.? Zwingli-Bücherei, no. 12. Zurich: Zwingli-Verlag, 1945.
307. "Ich glaube an eine heilige allgemeine apostolische Kirche." In *Auf dem Grunde der Apostel und Propheten. Festgabe für Landesbischof D. Theophil Wurm zum 80. Geburtstag am 7. Dezember 1948*, 119–31. Stuttgart: Quell-Verlag der evang. Gesellschaft, 1948.
308. "Imago Dei." *Neue Schweizer Rundschau* 2 (1934).
309. "Impressions of A Trip Through Asia." *Christianity and Crisis* 10 (July 10, 1950): 90–92.
310. "Inspiration und Offenbarung. Vortrag." *Der Kirchenfreund* 61 (1927).
311. "Intellectual Autobiography." Translated by Keith Chamberlain. In *The Theology of Emil Brunner*, ed. Charles W.

Kegley, 3–20. The Library of Living Theology Series, no. 3, eds. Charles W. Kegley and Robert W. Bretall. New York: Macmillan Company, 1962.

312. "Is Jesus Coming?" *The Christian Century* 48 (December 23, 1931): 1621–23.
313. "Is Religion Really 'Idealistic' as the Marxists Declare?" *World Communique* 7 (1948).
314. "Is Religion Really 'Idealistic' as the Marxists Declare?" *Ceylon Men* 5 (May 1949).
315. "Is Religion Really 'Idealistic' as the Marxists Declare?" *Manhood: Y.M.C.A. National Magazine* 3 (1948).
316. "Ist Christus zerteilt?" In *Zwinglikalender 1944*. Basel: Reinhardt, 1944.
317. "Ist die sogen Kritische Theologie wirklich Kritisch?" In *Kirchenblatt für die reformierte Schweiz*. 36 (1923).
318. "Is there a personal relationship to Jesus Christ?" *World Communique* 7 (1948).
319. "Japanese Christianity." *The Christian Century* 72 (May 25, 1955): 622–24.
320. "Japan heute." *Schweizer Monatshefte* 14 (1955).
321. "Japan in der Entscheidung. Interview von Pfr. Dr. P. Vogelsanger mit Emil Brunner." *Reformatio* 5 (1956).
322. "Japanische Reiseeindrücke I." *Neue Zürcher Zeitung* (October 1948).
323. "Japanische Reiseeindrücke II." *Neue Zürcher Zeitung* (November 1948).
324. "Japanische Reiseeindrücke III." *Neue Zürcher Zeitung* (December 1948).
325. "50 Jahre Libertas. Jubiläumsansprache." *Die Junge Schweiz*. 19 (1943).
326. "75 Jahre Schweiz. Ostasien-Mission." *Ostasien. Mitteilungen der Schweiz Ostasien-Mission* 75 (?1958).
327. "Jazz und Grammophon im Gottesdienst." *Kirchenblatt für die reformierte Schweiz*. 86 (1930).
328. "Je suis l'Eternel, ton Dieu." In *L'ordre de Dieu. La vie chrétienne à la lumière du décalogue*, 4–11. Geneva: Messager, 1941.
329. "Je suis l'Eternel, ton Dieu." In *L'ordre de Dieu. La vie chrétienne à la lumière du décalogue*, 2d ed., 5–20. Delachaux: Messager, 1946.

330. "John R. Mott, ein Pionier des Völkerfriedens." *Kirchenbote für den Kanton Zürich* 33 (1947).
331. "Zur Judenfrage." *Neue Schweizer Rundschau* 3 (?1935): 385–97.
332. *Zur Judenfrage.* Zurich: Fretz & Wasmuth, 1935.
333. "Die junge Schweiz-was wir von ihr erhoffen." *Junge Schweiz* 5 (1929).
334. *Justice and Freedom in Society. Stenographic Record of the Extension Lecture Series, given at Seiko Gakuin, Shinjuku, Tokyo. October 1954–February, 1955.* Tokyo: Institute of Educational Research and Service, International Christian University, 1955.
335. *Justice and the Social Order.* Translated by Mary Hottinger. London: Lutterworth Press, 1945. See notes under *Gerechtigkeit, eine Lehre von den Grundgesetzen der Gesellschaftsordnung.*
336. *Justice and the Social Order.* Translated by Mary Hottinger. New York: Harper & Brothers, 1945.
337. *Justice and the Social Order.* Translated by Mary Hottinger. London: Lutterworth Press, 1946.
338. *Justice and the Social Order.* Translated by Mary Hottinger. London: Lutterworth Press, 1949.
339. *Der Kampf des Christen in der Gegenwart.* Zurich: Zwingli-Verlag, 1940.
340. *Der Kanton Zürich in der mediationzeit, 1803–1813. Inauguraldissertation.* Zurich: Selnau, Leemann & Co., 1908.
341. "Kant's Schrift vom ewigen Frieden." In *Vom Krieg und vom Frieden (Festschrift Max Hüber)*, 29–39. Zurich: Berichthaus, 1944.
342. *Der Kapitalismus als Problem der Kirche.* Kirchliche Zeitfragen, no. 14. Zurich: Zwingli-Verlag, 1945.
343. "Der Kapitalismus als Problem der Kirche." *Der Grundriss* 6 (September/November 1944).
344. "Karl Barth's Alternatives for Liberal Theology: A Comment." *The Hibbert Journal* 59 (July 1961).
345. "Die Kergedanken der Reformation. Vortrag geh. an der Generalkonferenz des deutschschweiz. Hoffnungsbundes in der Stadtkirche Thun." *Pflugschar.* 19 (1926).
346. *Die Kirche als Frage und Aufgabe der Gegenwart. Vortrag, geh. im Kanonalzürcherischen Pfarrverein, 20. Mai 1934.*

Bern: Gotthelfverlag, 1934. Also published under the title *Um die Erneuerung der Kirche.*
347. "Kirche im Alltag." In *Kirche und Staat: 4 Vorträge in Fraumünster,* 3d ed., 29–32. Zurich: Leemann, 1937.
348. *Die Kirchen, die Gruppenbewegung und die Kirche Jesu Christi.* Berlin: Fürche-Verlag, 1936.
349. *Die Kirchen, die Gruppenbewegung und die Kirche Jesu Christi.* 2d ed.? Berlin: Fürche-Verlag, 1936. Published in English as *The Church and the Oxford Group.*
350. "Die Kirche sprict zur Welt." *Der Grundriss* 4 (1942).
351. "Die Kirche und das Übernationale." In *Kirche und Welt. Studien und Dokumente.* Vol. 3, *Die Kirche und das Staatsproblem in der Gegenwart,* 2d. engld. ed., 16–24. Geneva: Forschungsabteilung des Oekumenischen Rates für praktisches Christentum, 1935.
352. "Die Kirche und der Krieg." *Neue Schweizer Rundschau* 4 (1936).
353. "Die Kirche und die sozialen Forderungen der Gegenwart." *Glarner Nachrichten* (December 16, 1918)
354. "Die Kirche und die Todesurteile wegen Landesverrats." *Neue Zürcher Zeitung* (November, 1942).
355. "Kirche und Fersehen." *Schweizer Radiozeitung* 28 (1951).
356. "Kirche und Fernsehen." *Der Ruf* 95 (1953)
357. "Kirche und Staat." In *Kirche und Welt. Studien und Dokumente.* Vol. 3, *Die Kirche und das Staatsproblem in der Gegenwart,* 11–15. Geneva: Forschungsabteilung des Oekumenischen Rates für praktisches Christentum, 1934.
358. "Kirche und Staat." In *Kirche und Welt. Studien und Dokumente.* Vol. 3, *Die Kirche und das Staatsproblem in der Gegenwart,* 2d engld. ed., 11–15. Geneva: Forschungsabteilung des Oekumenischen Rates für praktisches Christentum, 1935.
359. "Kirche und Staat." In *Zwinglikalender 1939.* Basel: Reinhardt, 1939.
360. "Die Kirche unserer Tage." In *Schweizer Buch,* 72–77. Zurich: Schweizer Druck und Verlagshaus, 1938.
361. *Die Kirche zwischen Ost und West. Vortrag, gehalten an 20. Juni 1949 im Pfarrverein des Kantons Zürich.* Stuttgart: Evangelisches Verlagswerk, 1949.
362. "Zur kirchlichen Lage in Deutschland." *Kirchenblatt für die reformierte Schweiz.* 103 (1947).

363. "Vom Kommunismus." In *Zwinglikalender 1952*. Basel: Reinhardt, 1952.
364. "Kommunismus, Kapitalismus und Christentum." *Christ und Welt* 1 (1948). This is an excerpt from the book of the same name.
365. *Kommunismus, Kapitalismus und Christentum*. Kirkliche Zeitfragen, no. 23. Zurich: Zwingli-Verlag, 1948.
366. "Der konfessionelle Frieden in der Schweiz." *Neue Zürcher Zeitung* (April 1940).
367. "Konservativ oder Radikal?" *Neue Wege* 12 (1918): 55–70.
368. "Die Krisis der Religion." In *Kirchenblatt für die reformierte Schweiz*. 37 (1922).
369. "Die Krisis in Protestantismus." *Süddeutsche Monatshefte* 19 (1928).
370. *Zur Lage und Aufgabe der Kirche in der Gegenwart*. Zurich: Zwingli-Verlag, 1940.
371. *Die Lehre vom Heiligen Geiste*. Kirchliche Zeitfragen, no. 15. Zurich: Zwingli-Verlag, 1945.
372. "Die Lehre vom Heiligen Geist. Referat, geh. an der 84. Versammlung des Schweiz. Ref. Pfarrvereins, 25.–27. Sept. 1944 in Luzern." In *Verhandlungen des Schweizerischen Reformierten Pfarrvereins*, 26–53. Lucerne: Buchdruckerei C. J. Bucher AG, 1944.
373. *Die Lehre vom Heiligen Geist. Referat, geh. an der 84. Versammlung des Schweiz. Ref. Pfarrvereins, 25.–27. Sept. 1944 in Luzern*. Kirchliche Zeitfragen, no. 15. Zurich: Zwingli-Verlag, 1945.
374. *The Letter to the Romans: A Commentary*. Translated by H. A. Kennedy. London: Lutterworth Press, 1959.
375. *The Letter to the Romans: A Commentary*. Translated by H. A. Kennedy. Philadelphia: Westminster Press, 1959.
376. "Liebesbund oder Ehe." In *Ins Leben hinaus*. Schriftenreihe der Jungbürgerinnen, no. 5, 7–9. Bern: Paul Haupt, 1945.
377. *Die Machtfrage*. Zurich: Zwingli-Verlag, 1938.
378. "Mädchenbund. Stimmen zur Frauenbewegung." *Korrespondenzblatt studierender Abstinenten* 22 (1918).
379. "Man and Technics–Whither? An Address to the Union of Technicians at Stockholm." *The Christian Newsletter* Supplement to 302 (?January, 1948), 7–16.
380. *Man in Revolt: A Christian Anthropology*. Translated by Olive Wyon. Lutterworth Library, no. 10. London: Lutterworth

Press, 1939. See notes under *Der Mensch in Widerspruch: Die christliche Lehre vom Wahren und vom Wirklichen Menschen*.

381. *Man in Revolt: A Christian Anthropology*. Translated by Olive Wyon. New York: Charles Scribner's Sons, 1939.
382. *Man in Revolt: A Christian Anthropology*. Translated by Olive Wyon. Philadelphia: Westminster Press, 1947.
383. *Man in Revolt: A Christian Anthropology*. Translated by Olive Wyon. London: Lutterworth Press, 1948.
384. *Man in Revolt: A Christian Anthropology*. Translated by Olive Wyon. Lutterworth Library, no. 10. London: Lutterworth Press, 1939; reprint, London: Lutterworth Press, 1962.
385. "Martin Luther geh. Ansprache über den Landessender Beromünster." *Reformierte Schweiz* 3 (1946).
386. "Max Huber zum siebzigsten Geburtstag." *Neue Schweizer Rundschau* 12 (1945).
387. *The Mediator: A Study of the Central Doctrine of the Christian Faith*. Translated by Olive Wyon. New York: Macmillan Company, 1934. Translation of the 2nd edition, 1932, of *Der Mittler*. See notes under that title.
388. *The Mediator: A Study of the Central Doctrine of the Christian Faith*. Translated by Olive Wyon. London: Religious Tract Society, 1934.
389. *The Mediator: A Study of the Central Doctrine of the Christian Faith*. Translated by Olive Wyon. Lutterworth Library, no. 3. London: Lutterworth Press, 1934. First English version. Based upon unaltered text of 1st German edition of *Der Mittler*.
390. *The Mediator: A Study of the Central Doctrine of the Christian Faith*. Translated by Olive Wyon. Lutterworth Library, no. 3. London: Lutterworth Press, 1937.
391. *The Mediator: A Study of the Central Doctrine of the Christian Faith*. Translated by Olive Wyon. Lutterworth Library, no. 3. London: Lutterworth Press, 1942.
392. *The Mediator: A Study of the Central Doctrine of the Christian Faith*. Translated by Olive Wyon. Lutterworth Library, no. 3. London: Lutterworth Press, 1946.
393. *The Mediator: A Study of the Central Doctrine of the Christian Faith*. Translated by Olive Wyon. Philadelphia: Westminster Press, 1947. Translation of the 2nd edition, 1932, of *Der Mittler*.
394. *The Mediator: A Study of the Central Doctrine of the Chris-*

tian Faith. Translated by Olive Wyon. Lutterworth Library, no. 3. London: Lutterworth Press, 1947.

395. *The Mediator: A Study of the Central Doctrine of the Christian Faith.* Translated by Olive Wyon. Lutterworth Library, no. 3. London: Lutterworth Press, 1949.

396. *The Mediator: A Study of the Central Doctrine of the Christian Faith.* Translated by Olive Wyon. Lutterworth Library, no. 3. London: Lutterworth Press, 1952.

397. *The Mediator: A Study of the Central Doctrine of the Christian Faith.* Translated by Olive Wyon. Lutterworth Library. London: Lutterworth Press, 1934; reprint, London: Lutterworth Press, 1963.

398. *The Mediator: A Study of the Central Doctrine of the Christian Faith.* Translated by Olive Wyon. Philadelphia: Westminster Press, 1947; reprint, Philadelphia: Westminster Press, 1965. Translation of the 2nd edition, 1932, of *Der Mittler.*

399. "Meditation: Christ Divided?" *Japan Christian Quarterly* 18 (Winter 1952) 4–6.

400. "Meine Begegnung mit der Oxforder Gruppenbewegung." *Kirchenblatt für die reformierte Schweiz.* 22 (1932).

401. "Meine Begegnung mit der Oxforder Gruppenbewegung." *Kirchenblatt für die reformierte Schweiz.* ?88 (1932).

402. *Meine Begegnung mit der Oxforder Gruppenbewegung.* Basel: Friedrich Reinhardt, 1933.

403. "Das Menschenbild und die Menschenrechte." *Universitas* 2 (1947). Originally entitled "Die Menschenrechte nach reformierter Lehre."

404. "Die Menschenrechte nach reformierter Lehre. Festrede des Rektors, gehalten an der 109 Stiftungs-feier der Universität Zürich, am 29 April 1942." In *Jahresbericht 1941/42,* 3–22. Zurich: Orell Fussli, 1942.

405. "Menschheit, Technik-wohin?" *Neue Schweizer Rundschau* 16 (1949).

406. *Der Mensch in Widerspruch: Die christliche Lehre vom Wahren und vom Wirklichen Menschen.* Berlin: Fürche-Verlag, 1937. English translation: *Man in Revolt.* Brunner's thesis is that humans, even unbelievers, are always related to God, and are therefore always responsible to God, even though we are in revolt against God. Our humanity is a result of our being created in the image of God, which means we were created to live in a responsible, intimate relationship of trusting obedi-

ence to God. Even though we have lost the power to actually responsibly answer God, we are still under the obligation to do so. Our humanity remains intact because we, unlike any other creature, have this obligation to answer. Brunner argues he has no argument with the doctrine that salvation is solely by grace, but that humanity's responsibility must be maintained. This, he says, leads him to believe in general revelation.

407. *Der Mensch in Widerspruch: Die christliche Lehre vom Wahren und vom Wirklichen Menschen.* 3d ed.? Zurich: Zwingli-Verlag, 1941.
408. *Der Mensch in Widerspruch: Die christliche Lehre vom Wahren und vom Wirklichen Menschen.* 4th ed.? Zurich: Zwingli-Verlag, 1965.
409. "The Message from Abroad for John Calvin Translation Society." *Fukuin to Sekai* (1959).
410. "A Message to American Christians Explaining the Significance of the International Christian University in Japan." *The Watchman-Examiner* 40 (1958).
411. "A Message to the Plenary." In *Forward Together in Faith. Report of the Plenary Meeting of the World's Committee of the Young Men's Christian Association at Nyborg Strand, Denmark, 1950,* 84–88. Geneva: World's Committee of Young Men's Christian Association, 1950.
412. *The Misunderstanding of the Church.* Translated by Harold Knight. London: Lutterworth Press, 1952. Translation of *Das Misverständnis der Kirche*; see notes under that title.
413. *The Misunderstanding of the Church.* Translated by Harold Knight. Philadelphia: Westminster Press, 1953.
414. *Das Misverständnis der Kirche.* Zurich: Zwingli-Verlag, 1951. Brunner applies to the church his insight into the subject-object understanding of truth. He distinguished sharply between the church, an institution and the ekklesia, the assembly of believers. Brunner believed that "orthodoxy"—faith seen as assent to right doctrine—went hand in hand with sacerdotalism, the church seen as the institution which dispenses the means of salvation through its sacraments.
415. *Das Misverständnis der Kirche.* ?Deutsche Lizenzausgabe Series. Stuttgart: Evangelisches Verlagswerk, 1951.
416. *Das Misverständnis der Kirche.* 2d ed.? Zurich: Zwingli-Verlag, 1951.
417. *Die Mitte der Bibel. 2 Kor. 5, 17–21. Abschiedspredigt, gehal-*

ten am 21. August 1938 im Fraumünster. Zurich: Zwingli-Verlag, 1938.

418. *Der Mittler: Zur Besinnung über den Christusglauben.* Tübingen: Verlag J. C. B. Mohr (Paul Siebeck), 1927. A follow up to *Religionphilosophie evangelischer Theologie.* The former tried to set out the underlying philosophy of the neo-orthodox movement, while this was intended as an actual specimen of the new theology. It deals with Christ's work as the mediator between God and man. In this work Brunner dealt first with the person of Christ, and then his work. Two decades later, in the second volume of his systematic theology, he reversed the order, arguing that we discover who Christ is on the basis of what he did, not the other way around.
419. *Der Mittler: Zur Besinnung über den Christusglauben.* 2d ed. Tübingen: Verlag J. C. B. Mohr (Paul Siebeck), 1930.
420. *Der Mittler: Zur Besinnung über den Christusglauben.* 3d ed. Tübingen: Verlag J. C. B. Mohr (Paul Siebeck), 1937.
421. *Der Mittler: Zur Besinnung über den Christusglauben.* Zurich: Zwingli-Verlag, 1937.
422. *Der Mittler: Zur Besinnung über den Christusglauben.* Zurich: Zwingli-Verlag, ?1938.
423. *Der Mittler: Zur Besinnung über den Christusglauben.* 4th ed. Zurich: Zwingli-Verlag, 1947.
424. "Morgenandacht (über Eph. 4, 1–6), gehalten in der Wasserkirche vorgängig den Verhandlungen der Kirchensynode vom 9. Mai 1950." In *Protokoll der Kirchensynode des Kantons Zürich. 17 Amtsdauer. VI. Die Verhandlungen der ausserordentlichen Versammlung vom 9. Mai 1950,* 61–64. Zurich: n.p., ?1950.
425. "Die Mukyokai-Bewegung in Japan." In *Zwinglikalender 1956.* Basel: Reinhardt, 1956.
426. "Must I Believe in Jesus Christ?" *World Communique* 7 (1948).
427. "The Mystery of I Am." *The Pulpit: A Journal of Contemporary Preaching* 26 (May 1955): 5–7.
428. "The Mystery of Life." *World Communique* 7 (1948).
429. "The Mystery of Life." *Ceylon Men* 5 (January, 1949).
430. *Die Mystik und das Wort. Der Gegensatz zwischen moderner Religionsauffassung und christlichen Glauben dargestellt an der Theologie Schleiermachers.* Tübingen: Verlag J. C. B. Mohr (Paul Siebeck), 1924. Brunner strongly criticizes

Schleiermacher's theology and attacks classical liberal theology. This work clearly established Brunner as a scholar in his own right and was in large degree responsible for securing his appointment as a professor at the University of Zurich.

431. *Die Mystik und das Wort. Der Gegensatz zwischen moderner Religionsauffassung und christlichen Glauben dargestellt an der Theologie Schleiermachers.* 2d ed. Tübingen: Verlag J. C. B. Mohr (Paul Siebeck), 1928.

432. *Die Mystik und das Wort. Der Gegensatz zwischen moderner Religionsauffassung und christlichen Glauben dargestellt an der Theologie Schleiermachers.* Zurich: Zwingli-Verlag, 1938.

433. "Nachkriegsaufgabe der weitweiten Kirche." *Reformierte Schweiz.* 2 (1945).

434. "Im Namen Gottes des Allmächtigen, 1291–1941." In *Im Namen Gottes des Allmächtigen, 1291–1941*, 31–42. Zurich: Verlag der Jungen Kirche, 1941.

435. "Im Namen Gottes des Allmächtigen, 1291–1941." *Der Grundriss* 3 (1941).

436. ?*Nature and Grace*. London: University Microfilms Limited, 1959. ?p. 15–64 of the 1946 *Natural Theology* . . . volume of Geoffrey Bles, The Centenary Press.

437. *Natur und Gnade: Zum Gespräch mit Karl Barth*. Tübingen: Verlag J. C. B. Mohr (Paul Siebeck), 1934. Continuing fascination with anthropology led Brunner to the issue of natural theology. This resulted in a serious rift with Karl Barth brought about by Brunner's publication of this work, in which he argues for a limited natural theology.

438. *Natur und Gnade: Zum Gespräch mit Karl Barth*. 2d enlgd. ed. Tübingen: J. C. B. Mohr, 1935.

439. *Natur und Gnade: Zum Gespräch mit Karl Barth*. 2nd enlgd. ed. Zurich: Zwingli-Verlag, 1938.

440. *Natur und Gnade: Zum Gespräch mit Karl Barth*. Zurich: Zwingli-Verlag, ?1953.

441. "De-Nazification to Re-Nazification." *Motive* 8 (1947): 29–30.

442. *Vom Neuanfangen Predigt.* Zurich: Zwingli-Verlag, 1940.

443. "Der Neue Barth: Bermerkungen zu Karl Barths Lehre über Menschen." *Zeitschrift für Theologie und Kirche* 48 (1951): 89–100.

444. "The New Barth: Observations on Karl Barth's Doctrine of Man." *Scottish Journal of Theology* 4 (June 1951): 123–135.

445. *The New Barth: Observations on Karl Barth's Doctrine of Man.* n.p.: n.p.: 1951. This was reprinted from the *Scottish Journal of Theology.*
446. "Das Nichts oder Gott. Sonderheft: Die Bedrohung des Menschen heute. Vörtrage des Schweiz. evang. Akademikertages in Zürich." *Reformatio* 6 (1957). Also published under the title "Die Bedrohung des Menschen und der lebendige Gott."
447. *Die Offenbarung als Grund und Gegenstand der Theologie. Antrittsrede an der Universität Zürich, 17 Januar 1925.* Zurich: Zwingli-Verlag, 1938.
448. *Offenbarung und Vernunft: Die Lehre von der christlichen Glaubenserkenntnis.* Zurich: Zwingli-Verlag, 1941. Translated into English under the title: *Revelation and Reason.* The work was intended as a prolegomenon to the later three volume systematic theology. The book argues that reason must be subordinated to revelation if humans are to rightly understand God and themselves. It is also noteworthy for its effort to establish the proper relationship between faith, understood as trusting obedience, and doctrine.
449. *Offenbarung und Vernunft: Die Lehre von der christlichen Glaubenserkenntnis.* Zurich: Zwingli-Verlag, 1941; reprint, Zurich: Zwingli-Verlag, 1961.
450. *Ein offenes Wort an die Männer und Frauen von Obstalden und Filzbach. Zum Bettag 1917.* Obstalden: Selbstverlag, 1917.
451. *Ein offenes Wort; eingefuhrt und ausgewählt von Rudolf Wehrli*, Edited by Rudolf Wehrli. Zuok-Zürich: Theologischer Verlag, 1981.
452. "One Holy Catholic Church." Translated by Bruce M. Metzger. *Theology Today* 4 (October 1947): 318–31.
453. "An Open Letter." *World Communique* 8 (1949).
454. "An Open Letter. Democracy and Christianity." *World Communique* 8 (1949).
455. *L'Ordre de Dieu; la vie Chrétienne selon le Décalogue.* 2d ed. Collection L'Actualité Protestante. n.p.: ?Neuchatel, Delachaux et Niestle, 1946.
456. *Ostergewissheit. Predigt.* Zurich: Zwingli-Verlag, 1940.
457. "Ostern." *Neue Zürcher Zeitung* (April 1956).
458. *Our Faith.* Translated by John W. Rilling. New York: Charles Scribner's Sons, 1936. See notes under German title, *Unser Glaube.*

459. *Our Faith*. Translated by John W. Rilling. London: SCM Press Ltd., 1936.
460. *Our Faith*. Translated by John W. Rilling. London: SCM Press Ltd., 1936; reprint, London: SCM Press Ltd., 1949.
461. *Our Faith*. Translated by John W. Rilling. New York: Charles Scribner's Sons, 1936; reprint, New York: Charles Scribner's Sons, 1949.
462. *Our Faith*. Translated by John W. Rilling. London: SCM Press Ltd., 1936; reprint, London: SCM Press Ltd., 1950.
463. *Our Faith*. Translated by John W. Rilling. London: SCM Press Ltd., 1936; reprint, London: SCM Press Ltd., 1951.
464. *Our Faith*. Translated by John W. Rilling. New York: Charles Scribner's Sons, 1936; reprint, New York: Charles Scribner's Sons, 1954.
465. *Our Faith*. Translated by John W. Rilling. Toronto: S. J. R. Saunders, 1963.
466. *Our Faith*. Translated by John W. Rilling. New York: Charles Scribner's Sons, 1936; reprint, New York: Charles Scribner's Sons, 1962.
467. *Our Faith*. Translated by John W. Rilling. New York: Charles Scribner's Sons, 1936; reprint, New York: Charles Scribner's Sons, 1963.
468. "Pazifismus als Kriegsursache." *Neue Bünder Zeitung* 82 (May 1958).
469. "Pazifismus als Kriegsursache." *Neue Zürcher Zeitung* (April 1958).
470. *The Peace Message of the Church*. n.p.: n.p., n.d.
471. "Persönlichkeit und Person." In *Festschrift zu Ehren von Alt Rektor Dr. Hans Fischer, veröffentlich anlässlich des 50 jährigen Bestehens des Gymnasiums Biel*, 7–10. Biel: Graphische Anstalt Schüler A. G., 1952.
472. "Pestalozzi, der Christ." *Neue Zürcher Zeitung* (December 1940). A review of Karl Wurzburger's *Der Angefochtene, ein Buch uber Heinrich Pestalozzi*.
473. "Peter Winteler zum 70. Geburtstag." *Der Fürsorger. Mitteilungsblatt des Verbandes Schweiz. Fürsorger für Alkolohlgefährdete* 24 (1956).
474. "Pfingsten." *Neue Zürcher Zeitung* (June 1952).
475. *Philosophie und Offenbarung. Die Offenbarung als Grund und Gegenstand der Techologie. Antrittsrede an der Universi-*

tät Zürich, 17 Januar, 1925. Tübingen: Verlag J. C. B. Mohr (Paul Siebeck), 1925.
476. *Philosophie und Offenbarung. Die Offenbarung als Grund und Gegenstand der Techologie. Antrittsrede an der Universität Zürich, 17 Januar, 1925.* Zurich: Zwingli-Verlag, 1938.
477. *The Philosophy of Religion from the Standpoint of Protestant Theology.* Translated by A. J. D. Farrer and Bertram Lee Woolf. International Library of Christian Knowledge, eds. William Adams Brown and Bertram Lee Woolf. New York: Charles Scribner's Sons, 1937. Published in German under the title *Religion philosophie Evangelischer Theologie.*
478. *The Philosophy of Religion from the Standpoint of Protestant Theology.* Translated by A. J. D. Farrer and Bertram Lee Woolf. International Library of Christian Knowledge, eds. William Adams Brown and Bertram Lee Woolf. London: I. Nicholson and Watson, 1937.
479. *The Philosophy of Religion from the Standpoint of Protestant Theology.* 2d ed. Translated by A. J. D. Farrer and Bertram Lee Woolf. London: James Clarke & Co. Ltd., 1958.
480. *The Philosophy of Religion from the Standpoint of Protestant Theology.* Translated by A. J. D. Farrer and Bertram Lee Woolf. Westport, Conn.: Hyperion Press, 1979.
481. "Die politische Verantwortung des Christen." *Der Grundriss* 6 (1944).
482. *Die politische Verantwortung des Christen.* Kirchliche Zeitfragen, no. 11. Zurich: Zwingli-Verlag, 1944.
483. "Prédestination et Liberté." *Revue d'Historie et de Philosophie Religieuses* 32 (?April–June, 1952): 83–96. From a conference at the University of London, March 7–8, 1949, that was translated from the German by H. Mehl.
484. "The Predicament of the Church To-day." In *The Predicament of the Church*, ed. A. D. Lindsay, 82–99. London: Lutterworth Press, 1944.
485. "Predigt über 2. Korinther 3, 17.18." In *Dank an Emil Brunner*, ed. Peter Vogelsanger, 21–25. Zurich: Zwingli-Verlag, 1966.
486. "The Present-Day Task of Theology." *Religion in Life* 8 (Spring 1939), 176–186.
487. "Professor G. Schrenk. Zum 70. Geburtstag." *Neue Zürcher Zeitung* (February 1949).

488. "Protestantismus und Tiefenpsychologie." *Universitas* 6 (1951).
489. "Psychologie und Weltanschauung. Vortrag in der philosophischen Gesellschaft Zürich, 13 Febr. 1928." *Neue Schweizer Rundschau* 22 (1929).
490. "Qu'est-ce qu'une église vivante? Extraits de la conférence donee au Synode de l'Eglise jurassienne, le 3 juin 1941 à Bienne." *Les cahiers protestants* 25 (1941).
491. *Ration de réserve*. Pages suisses, no. 7. Geneva: A. Kundig, 194?.
492. "Real Freedom." *World Communique* 7 (1948).
493. "Real Freedom." *Ceylon Men* 5 (July, 1949).
494. "Reflexionen über amerikanische Pfarrerausbildung." *Jahresbericht des zürcherisch-aargauischen Stipendienvereins für Theologiestudierende*. 78 (1939).
495. "Reformation und Gemeinschaft." *Der Grundriss* 2 (1940).
496. *Reformation und Romantik. Vortrag gehalten bei der Tagung der Luther-Gesellschaft in München am 18. Juli 1925. Unveranderte Wiedergabe von D. Emil Brunner*. Munich: Chr. Kaiser Verlag, 1925.
497. *Die reformatorische Botschaft und die Wirtschaftsfrage. Reformationsvortrag in der freien protestantischen Vereinigung St. Gallen*. Bern: Gotthelf-Verlag, 1933.
498. "Reformierter und katholischer Glaube." In *Zwinglikalender 1937*. Basel: Reinhardt, 1937.
499. *Die reformierte Staatsauffassung. Vortrag vor der Neuen Helvetischen Gesellschaft in Zürich*. Zurich: Rascher Verlag, 1938.
500. "Ein reformiertes Wort zur Feier des Marburger Religiongespräches. Vortrag, geh. in Marburg, 1929." *Neuwerk* 11 (1929).
501. "Ein reformiertes Wort zur Feier des Marburger Religionsgespräches. Vortrag, geh. in Marburg, 1929." *Reformiertes Kirchenblatt* 10 (1929).
502. "Reiseeindrücke aus Korea." *Neue Zürcher Zeitung* (December 1948).
503. "Religion oder Glaube?" In *Zwinglikalender 1926*. Basel: Reinhardt, 1926.
504. *Religionphilosophie Evangelischer Theologie*. Munich: Verlag R. Oldenbourg, 1927. Attempts to set out the underlying philosophy of the neo-orthodox movement.

505. *Religionphilosophie Evangelischer Theologie*. Munich: Verlag R. Oldenbourg, 1928.
506. *Religionphilosophie Evangelischer Theologie*. 2d ed. Munich: Verlag Leibniz, 1948.
507. "Religious Socialism in Switzerland." *The Social Preparation* 14/15 (1919/20).
508. "Remarks [by Brunner]." *Reformed Review* (January 1956): 32–34.
509. *Le Renouveau de l'Église*. Translated by J. E. Siordet. Paris: Editions Je Sers, n.d.
510. "Reply to Interpretation and Criticism." Translated by Marle Hoyer Schroeder. In *The Theology of Emil Brunner*, ed. Charles W. Kegley, 325–52. The Library of Living Theology Series, no. 3, eds. Charles W. Kegley and Robert W. Bretall. New York: Macmillan Company, 1962.
511. *Responsabilités et tâches de l'Eglise. Conférence, donnée le 30 octobre 1944 aux pasteurs de l'Eglise nationale vaudoise à Lausanne*. Translated by M. P. Coigny. Lausanne: Le Semeur Vaudois, 1944.
512. *Revelation and Incarnation: An Address Delivered at the Alumni-Faculty-Student Mid-Winter Retreat, Union Theological Seminary, February 6, 1939*. ?New York: n.p., ?1939.
513. *Revelation and Reason: The Christian Doctrine of Faith and Knowledge*. Translated by Olive Wyon. Philadelphia: Westminster Press, 1946. See notes under German title *Offenbarung und Vernunft: Die Lehre von der christlichen Glaubenserkenntnis*.
514. *Revelation and Reason: The Christian Doctrine of Faith and Knowledge*. Translated by Olive Wyon. London: Student Christian Movement Press Ltd., 1947.
515. *Revelation and Reason: The Christian Doctrine of Faith and Knowledge*. Translated by Olive Wyon. Philadelphia: Westminster Press, 1946; reprint, Wake Forest, N.C.: Chanticleer Publishing Company Inc., n.d.
516. *Revelation and Reason: The Christian Doctrine of Faith and Knowledge*. Translated by Olive Wyon. London: Lutterworth Press, 1947.
517. *Der Römerbrief: übersetzt und ausgelegt*. Kassel: J. G. Oncken Verlag, 1938.
518. *Der Römerbrief: übersetzt und ausgelegt*. Bibelhilfe für die

Gemeinde Neutestamentliche Reihe, no. 6. Hamburg: Schloessmann, 1938.
519. *Der Römerbrief: übersetzt und ausgelegt.* Bibelhilfe für die Gemeinde Neutestamentliche Reihe, no. 6. Stuttgart: J. G. Oncken Verlag, 1948.
520. *Der Römerbrief: übersetzt und ausgelegt.* Kassel: J. G. Oncken Verlag, 1938; reprint, Berlin: Evangelische Verlagsanstalt, 1950.
521. *Der Römerbrief: übersetzt und ausgelegt.* ?2d ed. Bibelhilfe für die Gemeinde. Kassel: J. G. Oncken Verlag, 1956.
522. "Roots and Fruit." *Manhood: Y.M.C.A. National Magazine* 3 (1948).
523. *Saat und Frucht: Zehn Predigten über Gleichnisse Jesu.* Bücher des neuen lebens, no. 2 Berlin: Fürche-Verlag, 1938.
524. *Saat und Frucht: Zehn Predigten über Gleichnisse Jesu.* 2d ed.? Zwingli-Bücherei, no. 48. Zurich: Zwingli-Verlag, 1946.
525. "Der Säkularismus als Problem der Kirche. Eingangsvortrag zu einer missionstheologischen Konferenz. Basel, Frühjahr, 1930." *Unser Blatt* 1 (1930). Translated into English as "Secularism as a Problem for the Church."
526. *The Scandal of Christianity: The Gospel as Stumbling Block to Modern Man.* London: Student Christian Movement Press Ltd., 1951. The Andrew C. Zenos Lectures at McCormick Theological Seminary in Chicago, 1946, and the Robinson Lectures, Trinity College, Glasgow, 1948. The book contains five chapters focusing on: historical revelation, the trinity, original sin, the mediator, and the resurrection. There is reference to this being translated back into German from English under the title *Das Aergernis des Christenums*, but no further information could be located.
527. *The Scandal of Christianity: The Gospel as Stumbling Block to Modern Man.* Philadelphia: Westminster Press, 1951.
528. *The Scandal of Christianity: The Gospel as Stumbling Block to Modern Man.* Richmond: John Knox Press, 1965.
529. *The Scandal of Christianity: The Gospel as Stumbling Block to Modern Man.* Richmond: John Knox Press, 1965; reprint, Atlanta: John Knox Press, 1978.
530. "Schicksal und Freiheit in christlicher Sicht." *Neue Schweizer Rundschau* 5 (1938).
531. "Schöpfung und Technik. Predigt zum Jubiläum der Eidg.

Techn. Hochschule im Grossmünster zu Zürich am 31. Okt. 1955." *Schweiz. Bauzeitung* 73 (1955).
532. "Schöpfung und Technik. Predigt zum Jubiläum der Eidg. Techn. Hochschule im Grossmünster zu Zürich am 31. Okt. 1955." *Reformatio* 5 (1956).
533. "Schwarz ist weiss." *Neue Zürcher Zeitung* (November 1944).
534. "Schweizer Freiheit und Gottesherrschaft. Vortrag am Bettag 1939 an der Landesausstellung." In *Dienste unserer Heimat*, no. 1. Zurich: Zwingli-Verlag, 1939.
535. "Secularism as a Problem for the Church." *The International Review of Missions* 19 (October 1930): 495–511.
536. "Ein seelsorgerlicher Brief." In *Zwinglikalender 1929*. Basel: Reinhardt, 1929.
537. "The Significance of the Old Testament for Our Faith." Translated by C. Unhau Wolf. *The Lutheran Church Quarterly* 20 (July 1947): 330–44.
538. "Simon der Zauberer." *Kirchenblatt für die reformierte Schweiz.* 87 (1931): ?8, 9–24.
539. "Vom Sinn der Arbeit." In *Völker an der Arbeit*, 11–15. Zurich: Max S. Metz Verlag A.G., 1951.
540. *La situation de l'église et sa mission présente.* Translated by Marcel Jaton. Paris: Editions Je Sers, 194?.
541. *La situation de l'église et sa mission présente.* Translated by Marcel Jaton. Geneva: Editions Labor, 194?.
542. "Sollen sie also untergehen? Ansprache vom 12. Nov. 1934, als Werbung für 'Kinderhilfe' ". *Gesundheit und Wohlfahrt* (1934).
543. "Soll ich meines Bruders Hüter sein?" *Kirchenbote für den Kanton Zürich* 42 (1956). An excerpt from *Der Alkoholismus und unsere Verantwortlichkeit.*
544. "Some Remarks on Reinhold Niebuhr's Work as a Christian Thinker." In *Reinhold Niebuhr: His Religious, Social and Political Thought*, ed. Charles W. Kegley, Robert W. Bretall, 27–33. The Library of Living Theology Series, no. 2, eds. Charles W. Kegley and Robert W. Bretall. New York: Macmillan Company, 1956.
545. *Sowing and Reaping: The Parables of Jesus.* Translated by Thomas Wieser. London: Epworth Press, 1964.
546. *Sowing and Reaping: The Parables of Jesus.* Translated by Thomas Wieser. Richmond: John Knox Press, 1964.

547. *Sowing and Reaping: The Parables of Jesus.* Translated by Thomas Wieser. Toronto: Ryerson Press, 1964.
548. "Zur Sozialethik." *Kirchenblatt für die reformierte Schweiz.* 85 (1929).
549. "A Spiritual Autobiography." *Japan Christian Quarterly* 21 (July, 1955): 238–44. This was the 4th lecture given at the Spring Conference of Kyodan-related missionaries at Yumoto, April 1, 1955.
550. "Sprachverwirrung und Sorachenwunder." *Der Grundriss* 5 (1943).
551. *Der Staat als Problem der Kirche.* Bern: Gotthelf-Verlag, 1935.
552. "Der Staat und das christliche Freiheitverständnis." In *Kirche und Welt. Studien und Dokumente.* Vol. 7 *Totaler Staat und christliche Freiheit,* 37–59. Geneva: Forschungsabteilung des Oekumenischen Rates für praktisches Christentum, 1937.
553. "Der Sündenfall und die alttestamentliche Wissenschaft." *Christliche Welt* 40 (1926): 994–998.
554. *Das Symbolische in der Religiosen Erkenntnis: Beiträge zu einer theorie des religiösen Erkennens.* Tübingen: Verlag J. C. B. Mohr (Paul Siebeck), 1914. Brunner's Doctor of Theology dissertation, University of Zurich. The degree was awarded in 1913. The dissertation was a study of symbolism in religious knowledge, a conscious attempt to "get beyond Schleiermacher" whose theology Brunner was rejecting.
555. "Eine Traurede." In *Zwinglikalender 1930.* Basel: Reinhardt, 1930.
556. "Technik und Religion. Vortrag, geh. vor der Generalversammlung des SIA am 22. Sept. 1945 in Zürich." *Schweiz Bauzeitung* 126 (1945).
557. "Theologie." In *Schriften der Mlle. Marie Gretler-Stiftung der Universität Zürich, Heft 1, Wissenschaft und Glaube,* 9–28. Erlenbach: Rentsch, 1944.
558. "Theologie und Gemeinde. Referat, geh. an der Jahresversammlung des Schweiz. Evangelisch-Kirchlichen Vereins in Frauenfeld, Herbst 1944." *Der Kirchenfreund* 79 (1945).
559. "Theologie und Gemeinschaft." *Neue Wege* 23 (1929).
560. "Theologie und Kirche." *Zwischen den Zeiten* 8 (1930): 397–420.
561. "Theologie und Ontologie–oder die Theologie am Scheide-

wege." *Zeitschrift für Theologie und Kirche* 12 (1931): 111–122.
562. *The Theology of Crisis*. New York: Charles Scribner's Sons, 1929.
563. *The Theology of Crisis*. New York: Charles Scribner's Sons, 1929; reprint, New York: Charles Scribner's Sons, 1930.
564. *The Theology of Crisis*. New York: Charles Scribner's Sons, 1929; reprint, New York: Charles Scribner's Sons, 1933.
565. *The Theology of Crisis*. New York: Charles Scribner's Sons, 1929; reprint, New York: Charles Scribner's Sons, 1935.
566. "Theozentrische Theologie? Eine Bemerkung zu Schäders "Geistproblem der Theologie". *Zwischen den Zeiten* 4 (1926).
567. "Thoughts for Japan and for ICU." *Kokusai Kirisutokyo Daigaku Shimbun* (1959)
568. "Zur Todesstrafe." In *Zwei Stimmen aus der Kirche. Referate, geh. an der Kirchensynode am 28. Okt. 1942*, 19–26. Zurich: Zwingli-Verlag, 1942.
569. "Zur Todesstrafe." *Zofingue. Feuille centrale de la Société suisse de Zofingue* 92 (1952).
570. "Vom Tod und der Todesangst." *Zwinglikalender 1941*. Basel: Reinhardt, 1941.
571. "A Tribute to John MacKay." *Theology Today* 16 (1959).
572. *Truth as Encounter*. Translated by Amandus W. Loos, David Cairns and T. H. L. Parker. Engld. ed. of *The Divine Human Encounter* Philadelphia: Westminster Press, 1943. Philadelphia: Westminster Press, 1964. One of Brunner's most important works, originated as a series of lectures at the University of Uppsala, Sweden. Brunner argues that a right understanding of the gospel is hindered because Westerners, influenced by Hellenistic ideas, conceive of truth in terms of a subject-object antithesis. As a result we see truth as an abstract. Influenced by Buber and Kierkegaard, Brunner counters that in the Bible truth is always an encounter with God that changes the hearer. This understanding of truth became the pivot point for Brunner's theology for the rest of his life. The book itself was originally published in German as *Wahrheit als Begegnung*, Zurich: Zwingli-Verlag, 1938. It was first published in English as *The Divine-Human Encounter* in 1943. A second German edition of *Wahrheit als Begegnung* enlarged, with a new Part One, appeared in 1961. This volume is a translation of the second, reprinted edition, 1963 of

Wahrheit als Begegnung, enlarged with the new Part One. The new part was Brunner's last major undertaking, and in a sense closed the circle of his work, returning to the idea which underlay all his theological writing since the original publication, namely, the nature of truth itself as personal. The English translation of the first edition was by Amandus W. Loos. The translation of the new part and the corrections of the original English text were undertaken by David Cairns, in consultation with T. H. L. Parker.

573. *Truth as Encounter*. Translated by Amandus W. Loos, David Cairns, and T. H. L. Parker. The Preacher's Library. Enlgd. ed. of *The Divine Human Encounter* London: Student Christian Movement Press Ltd., 1944. London: Student Christian Movement Press, 1964.

574. *Truth as Encounter*. Translated by Amandus W. Loos, David Cairns, and T. H. L. Parker. Enlgd. ed. of *The Divine Human Encounter* Philadelphia: Westminster Press, 1943. London: Student Christian Movement Press Ltd., 1964.

575. *Truth as Encounter*. Translated by Amandus W. Loos, David Cairns, and T. H. L. Parker. Enlgd. ed. of *The Divine Human Encounter* Philadelphia: Westminster Press, 1943. Toronto: Ryerson Press, 1964.

576. "Das Uebernationale." *Neue Schweizer Rundschau* 2 (1934).

577. "Die Ueberwindung der Angst. Abendandacht." *Der Grundriss* 2 (1940).

578. "Das Unbedingte und die Wirklichkeit, unser Problem." *Neue Wege, Blatter für rel. Arbeit* 11 (1917).

579. "Unbekanntes Amerika." In *Zwinglikalender 1940*. Basel: Reinhardt, 1940.

580. "Und wenn der Kommunismus siegte . . . ?" *Kirche und Mann* (August 1961).

581. "Und wenn der Kommunismus siegte . . . ?" *Neue Zürcher Zeitung* (May 28 1961). Appears in English under the titles: "And Should Communism Be Victorious?" and "What If Communism Won Out?"

582. *Und wenn der Kommunismus siegte . . . ?* Schtiftenreihe des Schweizerischen Ost-Institutes, no. 6. Bern: Sager, 1961.

583. *Und wenn der Kommunismus siegte . . . ?* Zurich: Neue Zürcher Zeitung, 1961.

584. *Die Unentbehrlichkeit des Alten Testaments für die missionier-*

ende kirche. Vortrag am Basler missionsfest, 1934. Basler missionsstudien, no. 12. Stuttgart: Evang. Missionsverlag, 1934.
585. *Die unentbehrlichkeit des Alten Testamentes für die missionierende kirche.* 2d ed. Stuttgart: Evang. Missionsverlag, 1937.
586. "A Unique Christian Mission: The Mukyokai ("Non-Church") Movement in Japan." In *Religion and Culture: Essays in Honor of Paul Tillich*, ed. Walter Leibrecht, 287–290. New York: Harper & Brothers, 1959.
587. "The Uniqueness of the Y.M.C.A." *Ceylon Men* (April/May 1959). Same as "A Message to the Plenary. . . ."
588. "Die Unordnung der Welt und der Heilsplan Gottes." *Zwinglikalender 1949.* Basel: Reinhardt, 1949.
589. *Unser Glaube: eine christliche Unterweisung.* Zurich: Zwingli-Verlag, 1934. This work was eventually translated into nearly twenty languages. Small, non–technical, popular, and having widespread influence among laypeople, Brunner thought of this book as one of his most important.
590. *Unser Glaube: eine christliche Unterweisung.* Bern: Gotthelf-Verlag, 1935.
591. *Unser Glaube: eine christliche Unterweisung.* Bern: Gotthelf-Verlag, 1935; reprint, Bern: Gotthelf-Verlag, 1936.
592. *Unser Glaube: eine christliche Unterweisung.* Zurich: Zwingli-Verlag, 1934; reprint, Zurich: Zwingli-Verlag, 1940.
593. *Unser Glaube: eine christliche Unterweisung.* Zurich: Zwingli-Verlag, 1934; reprint, Zurich: Zwingli-Verlag, 1947.
594. *Unser Glaube: eine christliche Unterweisung.* Zwingli-Bücherei, no. 5. Zurich: Zwingli-Verlag, 1934; reprint, Zurich: Zwingli-Verlag, 1951.
595. *Unser Glaube: eine christliche Unterweisung.* Zurich: Zwingli-Verlag, 1934; reprint, Zurich: Zwingli-Verlag, 1958.
596. "Until Christ Be Formed in You—Excerpt from a Christmas Sermon." *Theology Today* 12 (January, 1956): 434–5.
597. [Various Answers.] In *Last Chance: Eleven Questions on Issues Determining Our Destiny*, ed. Clara Urquhart, 66, 81, 89, 90, 101, 109, 111, 120, 131, 141, 149, 159. Boston: Beacon Press, 1948.
598. "Verantwortlichkeit." In *Festschrift Heinrich Zangger*, 1000–7. Zurich: Rascher, 1935.
599. "Verheissung und Erfüllung." *Der Kirchenfreund* 83 (1949).
600. *Der Vermächtnis Calvins: Vortrag bei der Calvinfeier im Grossmünster am 28 Juni 1936.* Bern: Gotthelf-Verlag, 1936.

601. "Verwirrung in Staathegriff." *Neue Zürcher Zeitung* (May 1944).
602. *Volk, Schweizervolk, höre des Herrn Wort! Eidgenöss. Dank-, Buss- und Bettag.* Berlingen, Switzerland: Traktat-Missionsgesellschaft, 1957.
603. "Volk und Kirche." *Zwinglikalender 1931.* Basel: Reinhardt, 1931.
604. *Vom ewigen Leben.* Zurich: Zwingli-Verlag, 1942.
605. *Vom ewigen Leben.* 2d ed.? Zurich: Zwingli-Verlag, 1951.
606. *Vom ewigen Leben.* 3d ed.? Zurich: Zwingli-Verlag, 1953.
607. "Vom Rätsel Mensch." *Gemeindeblatt für die ref. kirchgemeinden des Kantons Glarus* 13 (1926).
608. *Von den Ordnungen Gottes. Vortrag im Berner Münster.* Bern: Gotthelf-Verlag, 1929.
609. "Von der Mission des Bildes." *Aktualis* (May 1941).
610. "Wahre und fasche Begründung des Osterglaubens." In *Der historische Jesus und der Kerygmatische Christus. Beiträge zum Christusverständnis in Forschung und Verkündigung*, ed. Helmut Ristow and Karl Mattiae, ?181–87. Berlin: Evangelische Verlagsanstalt Berlin, 1960.
611. "Wahre und fasche Begründung des Osterglaubens." In *Der historische Jesus und der Kerygmatische Christus. Beiträge zum Christusverständnis in Forschung und Verkündigung*, ed. Helmut Ristow and Karl Mattiae, 181–87. Berlin: Evangelische Verlangsanstalt Berlin, 1960; reprint?, Berlin: Evangelische Verlagsanstalt Berlin, 1961.
612. *Wahrheit als Begegnung.* 2d. enlgd. ed. Zurich: Zwingli-Verlag, 1961. See notes under *Truth as Encounter*.
613. *Wahrheit als Begegnung.* 2d. enlgd. ed. Zurich: Zwingli-Verlag, 1961; reprint, Zurich: Zwingli-Verlag, 1963. See notes under *Truth as Encounter*.
614. *Wahrheit als Begegnung: sechs Vorlesungen über das christliche Wahrheitsverständnis.* Zurich: Zwingli-Verlag, 1938. See notes under *Truth as Encounter*.
615. *Wahrheit als Begegnung: sechs Vorlesungen über das christliche Wahrheitsverständnis.* Zurich: Zwingli-Verlag, 1938; reprint, Zurich: Zwingli-Verlag, 1941. See notes under *Truth as Encounter*.
616. *Wahrheit als Begegnung: sechs Vorlesungen über das christliche Wahrheitsverständnis.* Zurich: Zwingli-Verlag, 1938; reprint,

Berlin: Fürche-Verlag, 1938. See notes under *Truth as Encounter*.

617. *Wahrheit als Begegnung: sechs Vorlesungen über das christliche Wahrheitsverständnis*. Zurich: Zwingli-Verlag, 1938; reprint, Zurich: Zwingli-Verlag, 195?. See notes under *Truth as Encounter*.
618. *Das wahre Volk. Predigt am Reformationssonntag 1933*. Bern: Gotthelfverlag, 1933.
619. "The War as a Problem of the Christian Church." *Christendom: An Ecumenical Review* 10 (September, 1945): 472–78.
620. "Warum allein Christus?" In *Zwinglikalender 1958*. Basel: Reinhardt, 1958.
621. *Warum Christus? Predigt*. Bern: Gotthelf-Verlag, 1936.
622. *Warum? Flugblatt, enthaltend eine religiöse Betrachtung zum Kriegsanfang*. Zurich: ?, 1939.
623. "Warum wir nach Japan gehen?" *Kirchenbote für den Kanton Zürich*. 39 (1953).
624. "Was bedeutet das Werk auf der Mainau vom standort der Gemeinde aus?" *Die Glocke* 3 (1949).
625. *Was hat Amerika uns, was haben wir Amerika zu geben? Vortrag vor der Swiss American Society for Cultural Relations*. Swiss-American Society for Cultural Relations Publications Series, no. 4. Zurich: Schulthess & Co., 1945.
626. "Was heisst: Erbaut auf dem Grunde der Apostel und Propheten?" *Verhandlungen der Schweiz. ref. Predigergesellschaft* (1925): 34–53.
627. "Was ist Kirche?" In *Zwinglikalender 1953*. Basel: Reinhardt, 1953.
628. "Was ist und was will die sogenannte Oxford gruppe?" In *Zwinglikalender 1935*. Basel: Reinhardt, 1935.
629. "Was nachher? Betrachtung über das ewige Leben." *Kirchenbote für den Kanton Zürich* 41 (1949).
630. *Was sollen wir tun? Predigt*. Bern: Gotthelf-Verlag, 1936.
631. "Auf dem Wege zur Eneuerung der Kirche." *Der Schweizerspiegel* 34 (1959).
632. "Die Weihe zum heiligen Kreig. Festpredigt zur Einsegnungsfeier im Münster." In *Lasset uns halten an dem Bekenntnis der Hoffnung. Vom 126. Jahresfest der Basler Mission*. Basel: Basler Missionsbuchhandlung, 1941.

633. *Weihnachtsgruss an alle Gruppenfreunde der Schweiz, mit Theo Spörri.* Zurich: Fretz, 1936.
634. *Weihnachtspredigt über 2 Kor. 4, 6–7.* Zurich: Zwingli-Verlag, 1938.
635. "Welt und Person." *Zwinglikalender 1962.* Basel: Reinhardt, 1962.
636. *Vom Werk des heiligen Geistes.* Tübingen: Verlag J. C. B. Mohr (Paul Siebeck), 1935.
637. *Vom Werk des heiligen Geistes.* Zurich: Zwingli-Verlag, 1941.
638. "What if Communism Won Out?" *Christian Economics* 13 (September 1961).
639. "What if Communism Won Out?" *Swiss Review of World Affairs* 11 (July 1961): ?2–3. This and preceding item are both translations of "Und wenn der Kommunismus siegte . . . ?"
640. "Why I Returned to Japan (Interview by James A. Scherer)." *Japan Christian Quarterly* 20 (January, 1954): 14–17.
641. "Why Say Men are Born Sinners?" *World Communique* 7 (1948).
642. "Der wiedergefundene Bauplan." In *Zwinglikalender 1927.* Basel: Reinhardt, 1927.
643. "Wie soll man das verstehen? Offener Brief an Karl Barth." In *Christliche Gemeinde im Wechsel der Staatsordnungen: Dokumente einer Ungarnreise,* ed. Karl Barth, 59–66. Zurich: Evangelischer Verlag, A. G. Zollikon, 1948.
644. "Wie soll man das verstehen? Offener Brief an Karl Barth." *Kirchenblatt für die reformierte Schweiz.* 104 (1948).
645. "Wir Christen und unser Staat." In *Zwinglikalender 1942.* Basel: Reinhardt, 1942.
646. "Wo is nun dein Gott?" In *Zwinglikalender 1948.* Basel: Reinhardt, 1948.
647. "Worauf es ankommt." *Glarner Nachrichten* (March 3, 1919).
648. "The YMCA—Success or Failure?" In *Work Book of the 5th Asian Y.M.C.A. Leaders' Conference, 16th–25th April, 1959, at Gotemba, Japan.* ?Japan: n.p., ?1959. Same as "A Message to the Plenary. . . ."
649. "Zum wirtschaftlich-sozialen Problem." *Neue Zürcher Zeitung* (March 1946).
650. "Wissenschaft und Glaube. Vortrag anl. der Generalversammlung des Technischen Vereins Winterthur." *Neues Winterthurer Tagblatt* (December 1944): 23–29.

651. *The Word and the World.* London: Student Christian Movement Press Ltd., ?1931.
652. *The Word and the World.* New York: Charles Scribner's Sons, 1931.
653. *The Word and the World.* 2d ed. London: Student Christian Movement Press Ltd., 1932.
654. *The Word and the World.* London: Student Christian Movement Press, 1931; reprint, Lexington, Kentucky: American Theological Library Association, 1965.
655. *The Word of God and Modern Man.* Translated by David Cairns. Richmond: John Knox Press, 1964. See notes under *Das Wort Gottes und der moderne Mensch.*
656. *The Word of God and Modern Man.* Translated by David Cairns. London: Epworth Press, 1965.
657. "A Word to the Christians in Japan." *Fukuin to Sekai* (1959).
658. "Ein Wort der Zürcher Kirche zur Ehefrage." In *Auftrag der Zürcher Kirchensynode, herausgegeben vom Kirchenrat des Kantons Zürich.* Zurich: Zwingli-Verlag, 1945.
659. *Das Wort Gottes und der moderne Mensch.* Berlin: Fürche-Verlag, 1937. A work of apologetics, published in English as *The Word of God and Modern Man.*
660. *Das Wort Gottes und der moderne Mensch.* Zwingli-Bücherei, no. 49. Zurich: Zwingli-Verlag, 1947.
661. "Das Wort ward Fleisch." *Leben und Glauben, Evangelisches Wochenblatt* 23 (1948).
662. "The Year in Europe." *World Communique* 62 (1952).
663. "Zaachaeus the Publican: A Sermon." Translated by Douglas Horton. *The Christian Century* 47 (March 26, 1930): 395–398.
664. "Zachäus der Zöllner. Predigt, geh. in der Kirche Oberstrass." *Zwischen den Zeiten* 6 (1928).
665. *Zeitliche Ordnung und Ewigkeitshoffnung: Vortrag gehalten am 9. April 1947 in Stuttgart und am 11. April auf der Theol. Woche in Willingen/Waldeck.* Schriftenreihe Lebendige Wissenschaft, no. 5. Stuttgart: Kreuz-Verlag, 1948. This contains two sermons, viz.-"Die ernte ist gross, aber wenige sind der arbeiter" by Brunner, and "Es wird gepredigt werden das evangelium vom Reich" by Lüthi.
666. "Der Zorn Gottes und die Versöhnung durch Christus." *Zwischen den Zeiten* 5 (1927): 93–115.

667. "Zum Zeugnis für Dr. Gerstenmaier." *Neue Zürcher Zeitung* (July 1945).
668. "Zwanzig Jahre später." *Kirchenbote für den Kanton Zürich* 47 (1961).
669. "Der Zweck der Verkündigung." In *Sinn and Wesender Verkündigung. Vorträge anl. der 2. Studenten-Zusammenkunft in Gwatt*, 40–55. Zollikon: Evangelischer Verlag, 1941.
670. *Zwei Predigten über die Gerechtigkeit.* Zurich: Zwingli-Verlag, 1942.
671. "Zwischen Kommunismus und Kapitalismus." *Evangelische Welt. Nachrichtendienst der Evangelischen Kirche von Westfalen* (1948).
672. "Zwischen Scylla und Charybdis. (Betrifft Frage nach der Grundlage einer Lehre von den gerechten sozialen Ordnungen)." *Kirchenblatt für die reformierte Schweiz.* 100 (November 16, 1944): 354–56.
673. "Zwischen Scylla und Charybdis. (Betrifft Frage nach der Grundlage einer Lehre von den gerechten sozialen Ordnungen)." *Kirchenblatt für die reformierte Schweiz.* 100 (November 30, 1944): 372–76.

Works Edited by Brunner

674. *Religionsphilosophie protestantischer Theologie: Handbuch der Philosophie.* Munich: Verlag R. Oldenbourg, 1927.
675. *Religionsphilosophie protestantischer Theologie: Handbuch der Philosophie.* Munich: Verlag R. Oldenbourg, 1927; reprint, Munich: Leibnizverlag, 1948.

Works Written by Brunner Jointly with Others

676. Brunner, Emil, et al. "Do you see any hopeful basis of Protestant-Roman Catholic Church Unity? 25 Scholars' Views." *Christianity Today* 5 (October 10, 1960): 29–32, 34, 38.
677. Brunner, Emil, et al. "Moon Shot: Its Meaning to 25 Scholars." *Christianity Today* 3 (October 13, 1958): 25–27, 29–31.
678. Brunner, Emil, et al. *Wissenschaft und Glaube: Vorträge von Emil Brunner et al.* Erlenbach: E. Rentsch, 1944.

679. Brunner, Emil, Hans J. Rinderknecht, and Konrad Zeller. *Kirche und Schule.* Zwingli-Bücherei, no. 40. Zurich: Zwingli-Verlag, 1944.
680. Brunner, Emil, H. Grossmann, Rudolf Grob and Peter Barth. *Unser Bekenntnis zu Jesus Christus.* Zurich: Zwingli-Verlag, 1938.
681. Brunner, Emil, and L. Ragaz. "Von Gottesreich und Weltreich. Ein Gedankenaustausch." *Neue Wege* 9 (1915).
682. Brunner, Emil, and Karl Barth. *Natural Theology, Comprising "Nature and Grace" by Professor Dr. Emil Brunner and the reply "No!" by Dr. Karl Barth.* Translated by Peter Fraenkel. London: Geoffrey Bles, The Centenary Press, 1946.
683. Brunner, Emil, and Karl Barth. *Natural Theology, Comprising "Nature and Grace" by Professor Dr. Emil Brunner and the reply "No!" by Dr. Karl Barth.* Translated by Peter Fraenkel. London: Geoffrey Bles, The Centenary Press, 1946; reprint, London: G. Bles, 1956.
684. Brunner, Emil, Karl Barth, and Erich Studer. *Die ökumenische Aufgabe in den reformierten Kirchen der Schweiz: Vortrag gehalten an den Kirchlichen Tagung in Zürich-Wipkingen, am 14. März 1949, von Prof. Dr. Karl Barth. Mit den einleitenden Diskussionsvoten von Prof. Dr. Emil Brunner und Gymnasiallehrer Dr. Erich Studer.* Zurich: Evangelischer Verlag, 1949.
685. Brunner, Emil, and Mark Sunder-Rao. "Two Answers to One Question by Professor Emil Brunner of Zürich and Mark Sunder-Rao of Madras." *World Communique* 8 (1949).
686. Brunner, E., P. Althaus, V.A. Demant, et al. *Die Kirche und das Staatsproblem in der Gegenwart, mit Beiträgen von P. Althaus, E. Brunner, V.A. Demant, u.a. . . .* Geneva: Forschungsabteilung des Oekumenischen Rates für praktisches Christentum, ?1934.
687. Brunner, Emil and Walter Lüthi. *Zu einem Zeugnis über alle Völker; zwie Missionspredigten gehalten von Emil Brunner und Walter Lüthi.* Das Evangelium vom Reich; missionspredigten von schweizer pfarren, no. 1.

Prefaces and Forewords Written by Brunner

688. Preface to *God's Grace and Man's Condition*, by David Bryn-Jones. Rutland, Vermont: Charles E. Tuttle Company, 1954.

689. Preface to *Le Protestantisme tel que Rome le voit*, by Franz J. Leenhardt. Geneva: Labor, 1942.
690. "Vom Altestenamt." *Der Grundriss* 3 (1941).
691. "Vom Altestenamt." Foreword to *Kleinen Handbuch für Kirchenvorsteher*. Zurich: Zwingli-Verlag, 1941.

Book Reviews Written by Brunner

692. "Eine protestantische Heilige." *Neue Zürcher Zeitung* (June, 1961). Review of Amy Carmichael von Dohnavur's, *Eine mutter für indische Tempelkinder, nach dem Englischen des Bischof Frank Houghton*. Authorized German edition by Fritz Enderlin.
693. Review of *Der Begriff der "Dialektik" und die Anthropologie*, by A. Sannwald. In *Zwischen den Zeiten* 10 (1932): 564–67.
694. Review of *Der Gottesgedanke und der zerfall der Moderne*, by Friedrich Karl Schumann. In *Kirchenblatt für die reformierte Schweiz*. 85 (1929).
695. Review of *Der Römerbrief*, by Karl Barth. In *Kirchenblatt für die reformierte Schweiz*. 34 (1919). This is Brunner's review of Barth's famous Commentary on the Book of Romans, which marked the formal, public announcement of the birth of neo-orthodoxy. Brunner was very complimentary!
696. Review of *Eine Religionsphilosophie vom Standpunkt der Offenbarung*, by Oskar Bauhofer. In *Kirchenblatt für die reformierte Schweiz*. 87 (1931).

SECONDARY SOURCES: WORKS ABOUT BRUNNER

1. Akehurst, John Edward. "The Christology of Emil Brunner and Its Role within His Wider Theological System." Ph.D. diss., Boston University, 1975.
2. Allen, Edgar Leonard. *Creation and Grace: A Guide to the Thought of Emil Brunner.* New York: Philosophical Library, 1951.
3. Althaus, Paul. Review of *Wahrheit als Begegnung.* 2d ed. *Theologische Literaturzeitung* 90 (February 1965): 135–138.
4. Andelson, Robert Vernon. "Human Rights: A Typological Survey of Their Theoretical Foundations (With Special Reference to Rousseau, Bentham, and Brunner)." Ph.D. diss., University of Southern California, 1960.
5. Anders, Jarlert. "Pa vag mot en personalistisk ekumenik: Tva teologiska program i aktiv arbetsgenmenskap."*Kyrohistorisk arsskrift* 89 (1989): 133–148.
6. Arnold, John James. "A Study of Christologies of H. Emil Brunner and Gerrit C. Berkouwer." Ph.D. diss., Hartford Seminary Foundation, 1968.
7. Atwater, Warren Eastwood, Jr. "A Critical and Comparative Study of Conscience: A Study of the Theological Thought of Emil Brunner in Relation to the Psychoanalytic Thought of Sigmund Freud." Ph.D. diss., University of Chicago, 1970.
8. Aubrey, E. E. Review of *The Christian Doctrine of God; Dogmatics, Vol. 1,* by Emil Brunner. *Journal of Bible and Religion* 19 (July 1951): 148–150.
9. Bailey, William Henry. "Two Thinkers on Justice: A Comparison of the Thought of Kant and Brunner, An Attempt to Arrive at a Christian Conception of Law." Ph.D. diss., Temple University, 1960.
10. Barker, C. J. Review of *Truth As Encounter.* New enlgd. ed.

of *The Divine-Human Encounter*, by Emil Brunner. *Church Quarterly Review* 166 (July, 1965): 376–377.
11. Beaven, Robert H. "Personal Relations in the Thought of Buber and Brunner." Ph.D. diss., University of Chicago, 1955.
12. Benktson, Benkt-Erik. Review of *Band 3, Dogmatik. Die Christliche Lehre von der Kirche, vom Glauben und von der Vollendung*, by Emil Brunner. In *Theologische Zeitschrift* 17 (September–October, 1961): 377–379.
13. Bernard, Walter. "The Philosophy of Spinoza and Brunner." Ph.D. diss., New York University, 1933.
14. Bertram, Robert. "Brunner on Revelation." *Concordia Theological Monthly* 22 (September, 1951): 625–643.
15. Blake, Fritz, Max Huber, Werner Kagi, and Hendrik Kraemer, eds. *Des Menschenbild im Lichte des Evangeliums: Festschrift zum 60. Geburtstag von Prof. Dr. Emil Brunner.* Zurich: Zwingli-Verlag, 1950.
16. Blanshard, Brand. *Reason and Belief.* New Haven: Yale University Press, 1974.
17. ———. "Reason and Unreason in Religion." *Zygon* 1 (June, 1966): 200–204.
18. Bourne, Howard A. "The Economic Concepts of Emil Brunner and Reinhold Niebuhr." Ph.D. diss., University of Chicago, 1950.
19. Bowen, T. Hassel. Review of *I Believe in the Living God: Sermons on the Apostles' Creed*, by Emil Brunner. In *Intepretation* 15 (April, 1961): 239.
20. Boyd, Malcolm. "Point of Contact: Doctrinal Examination of Barth, Brunner, and Tillich on Revelation." *Anglican Theological Review* 39 (January, 1957): 70–81.
21. Bronkema, Frederick. "The Relation of Natural Theology to Revelation in the Thought of Emil Brunner." Ph.D. diss., Yale University, 1937.
22. Brooks, Gregory Keith. "Marriage as Covenant: A Constructive Response to Emil Brunner and Joseph Allen." Th.M. thesis, Southern Baptist Theological Seminary, 1988.
23. Brown, C. Review of *Dogmatics. Vol. 3: Christian Doctrine of the Church, Faith and the Consummation*, by Emil Brunner. In *The Churchman* 77 (December, 1963): 274–276.
24. Brown, Sandra Read. "Reconciliation in Pastoral Marriage Counseling: A Theological Study Linking the Concept of

Reconciliation in Light of Emil Brunner with Actual Case Studies of Pastoral Marriage Counseling." Ph.D. diss., Princeton Theological Seminary, 1980.
25. Brunner, Hans Heinrich. "Loyalitaet." *Reformatio* 35 (August, 1986): 261–266. This is a reprint from *Mein Vater und Sien Aeltester: Emil Brunner in Seiner und Meiner Zeit.*
26. ———. *Mein Vater and sein Altester: Emil Brunner in seiner und meiner Zeit.* Zurich: Theologischer Verlag Zurich, 1986. This volume written by Brunner's son, is the only published biography of Emil Brunner's life. It has, unfortunately, never been translated into English.
27. Bulman, James M. "A Comparison of John Calvin's and Emil Brunner's Doctrine of God." Ph.D. diss., Southern Baptist Theological Seminary, 1949.
28. Bryant, Robert H. "The theology of Emil Brunner: pro and con." *Christian Century* 81 (January 15, 1964): 81–84.
29. Buess, Eduard. "Probleme der Trinitaetslehre: im Spiegel neuerer darstellungen." *Theologische Zeitschrift* 9 (September–October, 1953): 354–371. A comparison of the views of Althaus, Brunner, and Vogel on the doctrine of the Trinity.
30. Buford, Thomas Oliver. "The Idea of Creation in Plato, Augustine, and Emil Brunner." Ph.D. diss., Boston University, 1963.
31. Burrington, Dale Eugene. "The Place of Natural Law in Protestant Ethics; An Examination of Emil Brunner's Ethical Theory." Ph.D. diss., Johns Hopkins University, 1966.
32. Butler, William Warren. "A Comparison of the Ethics of Emil Brunner and Dietrich Bonhoeffer with Special Attention to the Orders of Creation and the Mandates." Ph.D. diss., Emory University, 1970.
33. Cairns, David. "Theologians of Our Time: The Theology of Emil Brunner." *Expository Times* 76 (November, 1964): 55–58.
34. ———. "The Theology of Emil Brunner." *Scottish Journal of Theology* 1 (December, 1948): 294–308.
35. Camenisch, Paul Frederick. "Good Reasons for Judgments of Moral Obligation and Their Use in the Theological Ethics of Emil Brunner." Ph.D. diss., Princeton University, 1971.
36. Cauthen, Kenneth. "Biblical Truths and Rational Knowledge." *Review and Expositor* 53 (October, 1956): 467–76.
37. Chang, Andrew Dooman. "Crisis of Biblical Authority: A Critical Examination of Biblical Authority in Contemporary

Theology with Special Reference to Functionalism." Th.D. diss., Dallas Theological Seminary, 1985. Final part of dissertation includes a criticism of the "christological functionalism" of Barth and Brunner.

38. Chemparathy, George. "Dialetical Theology and Non-Christian Religions." *Dharma* 6 (October–December, 1981): 399–416. Well written article surveying the views of Barth, Brunner, and Johannes Witte on the nature of non–Christian religions as well as the relationship between Christianity and other religions. Points out that both Barth and Brunner were concerned, over against liberal theology to reemphasize the uniqueness of Christ and Christianity. But while Barth denied that there was any revelation of God whatever in religions other than Christianity, which should indeed not even be called religions, and taught that all such religions were in fact unbelief, Brunner took a much less harsh view. He believed there was some degree of revelation in all religions, particularly more so in some than others, though in no case was the revelation sufficient for salvation.

39. Clark, Issac Rufus. "Redemption in the Thought of Emil Brunner and Albert Cornelius Knudson." Th.D. diss., Boston University, 1958.

40. Cobb, William Daniel, III. "Moral Relativity and Christian Ethics: A Study in Response to the Theology of Emil Brunner and Reinhold Niebuhr." Ph.D. diss., University of Chicago, 1967.

41. Collins, Kenneth J. "Emil Brunner's twofold understanding of truth." In *Scholarship, Sacraments and Service: Historical Studies in the Protestant Tradition: Essays in Honor of Bard Thompson*, ed. Daniel B. Clendenin and W. David Buschart. Lewiston, New York: E. Mellen Press, 1990.

42. Cook, John. "Revised Reviews: Brunner's *The Divine Imperative*." In *Theology* 64 (August, 1961): 321–325.

43. Crowse, B. Merle. Review of *The Misunderstanding of the Church*, by Emil Brunner. In *Brethren Life and Thought* 5 (Summer, 1960): 64.

44. Cunliffe-Jones, H. Review of *Eternal Hope*, by Emil Brunner. *Church Quarterly Review* 32 (July, 1954): 264–65.

45. Danker, Frederick W. Review of *Letter to the Romans: A Commentary*, by Emil Brunner. In *Concordia Theological Monthly* 31 (April, 1960): 269–70.

46. Davies, J. G. Review of *Dogmatics. Vol 3: Christian Doctrine of the Church, Faith and the Consummation*, by Emil Brunner. In *Expository Times* 74 (March, 1963): 170–71.
47. Douglass, Herbert Edgard, Jr., "Encounter with Brunner: An Analysis of Emil Brunner's Proposed Transcendence of the Subjectivism-Objectivism Dichotomy in its Relation to Christian Proclamation." Th.D. diss., Pacific School of Religion, 1964.
48. Dyck, Arthur J. "Moral Requiredness: Bridging the Gap Between 'Ought' and 'Is' (Part 2)." *Journal of Religious Ethics* 9 (Spring, 1981): 131–150.
49. Eadie, Douglas G. "A Critique of Emil Brunner's View of Knowledge of God." Ph.D. diss., University of Southern California, 1954.
50. Eenigenburg, E. M. Review of *Dogmatics. Vol. 3: The Christian Doctrine of the Church, Faith and the Consummation*, by Emil Brunner. In *Reformed Review* 18 (March, 1965): 49–50.
51. Eccles, Robert S. Review of *Dogmatics. Vol. 3: Christian Doctrine of the Church, Faith and the Consummation*, by Emil Brunner. In *Journal of the Bible and Religion* 31 (July, 1963): 252–54.
52. Ehrhart, Carl Y. "The Conception of Imago Dei in the Thought of Emil Brunner." Ph.D. diss., Yale University, 1953.
53. Ehrlich, Rudolf J. Review of *Band 3, Dogmatik. Die Christliche Lehre von der Kirche, vom Glauben, und von der Vollendung*, by Emil Brunner. In *Scottish Journal of Theology* 14 (Spring, 1961): 295–97.
54. "Emil Brunner and the Wide Open Spaces." *Christian Century* 80 (February 20, 1963): 255. Short, complimentary editorial which neatly summarizes Brunner's life work as "working to close the wide-open spaces between church and pagan and showing the pagan how God closes the wide-open spaces between himself and the pagan."
55. "Emil Brunner Does It Again." *Christian Century* 78 (June 28, 1961): 790–91. Short editorial which criticizes Brunner's denunciation of consideration by the World Council of Churches of admission of Russian Orthodox Church, the Council's description of the horrors of nuclear war, and his complaint that the the Fifth World Order Study Conference remained silent on the dangers of communism.
56. Faber, Paul William. "Christian Belief and Divine Normative

Theories of Ethics." Ph.D. diss., University of Notre Dame, 1982. Includes brief review of Brunner's ethical theories.
57. Fangmeier, Jürgen. Review of *Wahrheit als Begegnung*, by Emil Brunner. In *Theologische Zeitschrift* 20 (January–February, 1964): 70–72.
58. Farley, Gary Eugene. "Authority in Contemporary Christian Ethics: A Study in How One May Know the 'Will of God' as Discussed in the Writings of Carl F. H. Henry, Jacques Maritain, Emil Brunner, Reinhold Niebuhr, and Nels F. S. Ferre." Ph.D. diss., Southwestern Baptist Theological Seminary, 1966.
59. Feijo, Olavo Guimaraes. "Two Biblical Cases of God-Man Relationship and Their Relevance for the Educative Process Analyzed According to the Existentialist Posture of Emil Heinrich Brunner [sic] and Van Cleve Morris." Ed.D., Southwestern Baptist Theological Seminary, 1970.
60. Fischer, Hermann. "Natuerliche Theologie im Wandel." *Zeitschrift für Theologie und Kirche* 80 (March, 1983): 85–102.
61. ———. "Systematische Theologie." In *Theologie im 20. Jahrhundert: Stand und Aufgaben*, ed. Georg Strecker, 289–388. n.p.: J.C.B. Mohr., 1983. Bibliographic essay, mentioning Brunner along with many others.
62. Furse, Margaret Lewis. "A Critique of Baron Von Hugel and Emil Brunner on Mysticism." Ph.D. diss., Union Theological Seminary, New York, 1969.
63. Furuya, Y. C. "Apologetic or Kerygmatic Theology?" *Theology Today* 16 (January, 1960): 471–480.
64. Gardner, Harry Miller. "The Doctrine of the Person and Work of Jesus Christ in the Thought of Peter Taylor Forsyth and of Emil Brunner." Th.D. diss., Boston University, 1962.
65. Geursen, M. W. J. "Nature and Grace." *Reformed Theological Review* 13 (February, 1954): 1–13.
66. Gibbs, M. E. "Christianity as A Historical Religion." *Indian Journal of Theology* 8 (1959): 10–20. Response to earlier article by K. C. Mathew.
67. Graby, James Kenneth. "The Significance of Friedrich Schleiermacher in the Development of the Theology of Emil Brunner, with Special Attention to the Early Period (1914–1929)." Ph.D. diss., Drew University, 1966.
68. Graham, Leroy Stoney. "An Examination and Analysis of the Relevance of the Christian Ethic of Sex with Respect to Premarital Sexual Intercourse: An Inquiry Based on the Thought of

Reinhold Niebuhr and Emil Brunner in View of the Findings of Alfred Kinsey and Margaret Mead." Ph.D. diss., Drew University, 1965.
69. Grant, M. Colin. "The power of the unrecognized 'blik': Adam and humanity according to Sören Kierkegaard and Emil Brunner." *Studies in Religion* 7 (no. 1, 1978): 47–52.
70. Griffith, Gwilym O. "Natural Theology and the Ministry of the Word." *Scottish Journal of Theology* 1 (no. 4, 1948): 258–71.
71. Guy, Fritz. "Differently But Equally: The Image of God: The Meaning of Womanhood According to Four Contemporary Protestant Theologians," in *Symposium on the Role of Women in the Church*, ed. J. Neuffer, 171–82. n.p., n.p.: 1984. This appears to be a work produced internally by the Seventh Day Adventist Church.
72. Harrison, M. H. Review of *Dogmatics. Vol. 3: Christian Doctrine of the Church, Faith and the Consummation*, by Emil Brunner. In *International Review of Missions* 53 (January, 1964): 118–121.
73. Hauge, Reidar. "Emil Brunners dogmatikk." *Norsk Teologisk Tidsskrift* 62 (no. 2, 1961): 81–101.
74. Hazelton, Roger. "Religion as Encounter." *Journal of Religious Thought* 14 (Spring–Summer 1957): 129–139.
75. Hedinger, Ulrich. "Kritische Bermerkungen zur Protologie." *Theologische Zeitschrift* 31 (March–April, 1975): 84–94.
76. Heideman, Eugene Paul. *The Relation of Revelation and Reason in E. Brunner and H. Bavinck*. Assen, Netherlands: Van Gorcum & Comp. N.V., 1959.
77. Hendry, George S. "An Appraisal of Brunner's Theology." *Theology Today* 19 (January, 1963): 523–531.
78. ———. Review of *The Christian Doctrine of God; Dogmatics, Vol. 1*, by Emil Brunner. *Theology Today* 7 (January, 1951): 535–538.
79. Hesselink, I. John. "Emil Brunner: A Centennial Perspective." *Christian Century* 106 (December 13, 1989): 1171–74.
80. ———. "Karl Barth and Emil Brunner—A Tangled Tale with A Happy Ending (Or, the Story of a Relationship)." In *How Karl Barth Changed My Mind*, ed. Donald K. McKim, 131–42. Grand Rapids, Michigan: W. B. Eerdmans Pub. Co., 1986. Interesting account of Hesselink's personal relationship with Brunner.

81. ———. Review of *Truth As Encounter*. New enlgd. ed. of *The Divine-Human Encounter*, by Emil Brunner. *Reformed Theological Review* 25 (January–April, 1966): 24.
82. Holder, Fred Lloyd. "Theology at the Crossroads: Ontology or Biblical Faith? A Critical Exposition and Evaluation of Rudolf Bultmann and Emil Brunner's Doctrine of Eschatological Existence in the Light of Their Theological Method." Ph.D. diss., University of Iowa, 1963.
83. Hollenweger, Walter. "Aus dem weltweiten Echo auf Emil Brunners Theologie." *Reformatio* 12 (August, 1963): 441–48.
84. ———. "Wurzeln der Theologie Emil Brunners (Aus Brunners theologischer Entwicklung von ca. 1913 bis 1918)." *Reformatio* 12 (October, 1963): 579–587.
85. Horton, W. M. "Divine Imperative." *Congregational Quarterly* 35 (January, 1957): 21–32
86. Hubbeling, Hubertus G. "Theological Portrait of Brunner." In *Bilanz der Theologie im 20sten Jahrhundert: Perspektiven Strömungen, Motive in der Christlichen und nichtchristlichen Welt*, vol. 4, ed. Herbert Vorgrimler and Robert Gocht, 65–80. Freiburg: Herder, 1969–1970.
87. Hudson, Thomas Preston. "The Concept of God as Personal in the Thought of John Baillie, Emil Brunner and Paul Tillich." Th.D. diss., New Orleans Baptist Theological Seminary, 1985.
88. Humphrey, J. Edward. *Emil Brunner*. Makers of the Modern Theological Mind Series, ed. Bob E. Patterson. Waco, Texas: Word Books, 1976. Excellent introductory work about Brunner. Includes a survey of major themes in his writing, and a helpful bibliography.
89. ———. *Emil Brunner*. Texas: Word Books, 1976; reprint, Peabody, Mass.: Hendrickson Publishers, 1991.
90. Hunt, B. Review of *Dogmatics. Vol. 3: Christian Doctrine of the Church, Faith and the Consummation*, by Emil Brunner. In *Southwestern Journal of Theology* 6 (October, 1963): 110–111.
91. Hynson, Leon O. "Theological Encounter: Brunner and Buber." *Journal of Ecumenical Studies* 12 (Summer, 1975): 349–366.
92. Idinpolulos, Thomas A. "Creativity and Christianity: A Polemic Based Upon Rudolf Bultmann, Emil Brunner, and Nicolas Berdyaev." Ph.D. diss., University of Chicago, 1966.
93. Irvine, Andrew R. "Isolation and the Parish Ministry." Ph.D. diss., University of St. Andrews, 1989. Based on extensive

survey of Church of Scotland clergy, the dissertation includes three chapters examining the self-separation from the perspective of Brunner and Tillich.
94. Jacobson, Sverre Theodore. "The Interpersonalism of Guilt and Forgiveness in the Writings of Harry Stack Sullivan and Emil Brunner." Ph.D. diss., Princeton Theological Seminary, 1959.
95. Jensen, Maud Keister. "The Missionary Motif in the Theology of Emil Brunner and Its Relation to Specific Doctrines." Ph.D. diss., Drew University, 1978.
96. Jensen, Vern Arthur. "Failure and Capability in Love: An Integrative Study of the Psychology of Erich Fromm and the Theology of Emil Brunner." Ph.D. diss., Drew University, 1966.
97. Jewett, Paul King. "Ebnerian Personalism and Its Influence Upon Brunner's Theology." *Westminster Theological Journal* 14 (May, 1952): 113–147.
98. ———. *Emil Brunner: An Introduction to the Man and His Thought*. Chicago: Inter-Varsity Press, 1961. Good introduction to Brunner and his thought, written from evangelical protestant perspective.
99. ———. *Emil Brunner's Concept of Revelation*. London: James Clarke & Co. Ltd., 1954.
100. ———. "Emil Brunner's Concept of Revelation." Ph.D. diss., Harvard University, 1951.
101. ———. "Emil Brunner and the Bible." *Christianity Today* 1 (January 21, 1957): 7–9.
102. Johnson, Wendell Gordon. "Soteriology as a Function of Epistemology in the Thought of Emil Brunner." Ph.D. diss. Rice University, 1989.
103. Kagi, Werner. "Gruss und Dank an Emil Brunner zum 75. Geburtstag, am 23. Dezember 1964." *Reformatio* 13 (December, 1964): 667–669.
104. Kegley, Charles W., ed. *The Theology of Emil Brunner*. The Library of Living Theology Series, eds. Charles W. Kegley and Robert W. Bretall, no. 3. New York: Macmillan, 1962. Important study of Brunner and his thought consisting of an "intellectual autobiography" written by Brunner, seventeen essays of "interpretation and criticism" by various theologians, and a reply by Brunner. Contains extensive bibliography.

105. Koch, T. "Natur und Gnade; zur neueren Diskussion." *Kerygma und Dogma* 16 (Fall, 1970?): 171–187.
106. Kutter, H. "Beitrag zur Rundfrage der Neuen Zürcher Zeitung. 'Die Schweiz in Buch'." *Neue Zürcher Zeitung* (April, 1927).
107. Leavenworth, James L. "The Use of the Scriptures in the Works of Emil Brunner." Ph.D. diss., Yale University, 1950.
108. Lee, Howard Douglas. "The Orders of Creation in the Ethical Theory of Emil Brunner." Ph.D. diss., University of Iowa, 1972.
109. Lehmann, Paul. Review of *Dogmatics. Vol. 3: Christian Doctrine of the Church, Faith and the Consummation*, by Emil Brunner. In *Union Seminary Quarterly Review* 19 (March, 1964): 256–258.
110. Lewis, H. D. "Revelation and Reason." *Hibbert Journal* 47 (1949): 56–64. Highly complimentary review of Brunner's *Revelation and Reason*.
111. Lewis, Hywel David. *Morals and the New Theology*. New York: Harper, 1947.
112. Lindsay, Sir Harry. "Creation from a New Angle: A Reply to Emil Brunner." *Hibbert Journal* 52 (1954): 368–374. Lengthy criticism of *The Christian Doctrine of Creation and Redemption* which argues that Brunner leaves unanswered "just those problems which puzzle the Christian layman." Argument wanders badly.
113. Little, John Frederick. "Amendment to Brunner's Concept of the Humanum." In *Ambulatio Fidei: Essays in Honor of Otto W. Heick*, ed. Erich R. W. Schultz, 30–41. Waterloo, Ontario: Walter Lutheran University, 1965.
114. ———. "The Role of Reason in the Apologetic Enterprise of Emil Brunner and Paul Tillich in Relation to the Myths of Genesis One to Three." Ph.D. diss., Princeton University, 1961.
115. Lovin, Robin W. *Christian Faith and Public Choices; the Social Ethics of Barth, Brunner, and Bonhoeffer*. Philadelphia: Fortress Press, 1984.
116. Marshall-Green, Molly Truman. "No Salvation Outside the Church? A Critical Inquiry." Ph.D. diss., Southern Baptist Theological Seminary, 1983. Devotes third chapter to Brunner's understanding of salvation outside Christ and the church, and offers an evaluation of same in the final chapter.

117. Martin, James Luther, Jr. "The Doctrine of Sin in the Theology of Emil Brunner and Reinhold Niebuhr." Ph.D. diss., Yale University, 1951.
118. Mathew, Karimpanamannil Chacko. "Radhakrishnan's and Brunner's Anthropologies: A Comparison." *Indian Journal of Theology* 6 (1957): 29–38, 67–73. Radhakrishnan was a prominent Indian philosopher, scholar and theologian, with particular interest in bringing Eastern and Western thought together.
119. ———. "Radhakrishnan's and Brunner's Anthropologies: A Comparison." Th.D. diss., Hartford Seminary Foundation, 1956.
120. McCool, Gerald A. "Recent Trends in German Scholasticism: Brunner and Lotz." *International Philosophical Quarterly* 1 (December, 1961): 668–682.
121. McIntyre, John. Review of *The Mediator*. *Reformed Theological Review* 16 (June, 1957): 11–20, 44–53.
122. McKim, Mark Gordon. "A Study of Emil Brunner's Criticism of Lutheran and Reformed Concepts of Faith." Th.D. diss. Boston University, 1993. Evaluation of Brunner's belief that the Reformers rediscovered the biblical concept of faith, but often lapsed back into the medieval conception of it as assent to right doctrine.
123. Micklem, C. Review of *The Christian Doctrine of God; Dogmatics, Vol. 1*, by Emil Brunner. *Church Quarterly Review* 28 (July, 1950): 271–272.
124. Mielke, Robert H. E. "The Doctrine of Imago Dei in the Theology of Emil Brunner." Ph.D. diss., Drew University, 1951.
125. Mikolaski, Samuel. "Some Reflections on *The Christian Doctrine of God*." *Evangelical Quarterly* 29 (April–June, 1957): 85–93.
126. Moellering, H. Armin. "Brunner and Luther on Scriptural Authority." *Concordia Theological Monthly* 21 (November, 1950): 801–18.
127. Moody, Dale. "An Introduction to Emil Brunner." *The Review and Expositor* 44 (July, 1947): 312–330.
128. ———. "The Problem of Revelation and Reason in the Writings of Emil Brunner." Th.D. diss., Southern Baptist Theological Seminary, 1947. Moody became a major Southern Baptist theologian. His writings showed considerable influ-

ence from Brunner. In the preface to the second volume of the dogmatics, Brunner refers to Moody as his "theological colleague."

129. ———. Review of *The Christian Doctrine of God; Dogmatics Vol. 1*, by Emil Brunner. *Review and Expositor* 49 (January, 1952): 63–64.

130. Moran, John W. *Catholic Faith and Modern Theologies: The Theology of Emil Brunner.* Worcester, Mass.: Heffernan Press, 1948.

131. Mueller, D. L. Review of *Dogmatics. Vol. 3: Christian Doctrine of the Church, Faith and the Consummation*, by Emil Brunner. In *Review and Expositor* 60 (Autumn, 1963): 445–448.

132. ———. Review of *Truth As Encounter*. New enlgd. ed. of *The Divine-Human Encounter*, by Emil Brunner. *Review and Expositor* 63 (Spring, 1966): 226–27.

133. Muller, Richard A. "Christ—The Revelation or the Revealer: Brunner and Reformed Orthodoxy on the Doctrine of the Word of God." *Journal of the Evangelical Theological Society* 26 (September, 1983): 307–19.

134. Murray, Noland Patrick. "Personalism in the Ethical Theory of Emil Brunner." Ph.D. diss., Duke University, 1963.

135. Nam, Kee Chul. "Two Types of Personalistic Interpretations of Man: Study of Albert C. Knudson and Emil Brunner." Ph.D. diss., Emory University, 1968.

136. Nelson, J. Robert. "Emil Brunner: Teacher Unsurpassed." *Theology Today* 19 (January, 1963): 532–535.

137. ———. Review of *Dogmatics. Vol. 3: Christian Doctrine of the Church, Faith and the Consummation*, by Emil Brunner. In *Encounter* 25 (Summer, 1964): 378–80.

138. ———. "Emil Brunner—The Final Encounter." *The Christian Century* 83 (April 20, 1966): 486.

139. Nicole, Roger R. "The Neo-orthodox Reduction." In *Challenges to Inerrancy: A Theological Response*, ed. Gordon Lewis and Bruce Demarest, 121–144. Chicago: Moody Press, 1984. Highly critical analysis of view of Scripture held by Barth and Brunner from the perspective of an evangelical scholar holding an inerrantist view of Scripture. Identifies Barth as the "foremost neo-orthodox leader" but incorrectly calls Brunner a "very influential follower."

140. Nordquist, Roger Frank. "Emil Brunner on the Province of Reason." Ph.D. diss., Yale University, 1966.

141. O'Donovan, Joan E. "Man in the Image of God: The Disagreement Between Barth and Brunner Reconsidered." *Scottish Journal of Theology* 34 (no. 4, 1986): 433–459.
142. Osoro, Robinson Ratemo. "Moral life, exemplars and critical reflection." Ph.D. diss., Michigan State University, 1990. Attempts to reconcile Brunner and Kurtz's views of the moral life.
143. Owen, Huw Parri. *Concepts of Deity*. London: Macmillan, 1971. Contains short section devoted to Brunner's conception of God.
144. Oyen, Hendrik Van. "Biblische Gerechtigkeit und Weltliches Recht." *Theologische Zeitschrift* 6 (July–August, 1950): 270–92.
145. Pennington, Chester Arthur. "The Essentially Wesleyan Form of the Doctrine of Redemption in the Writings of Emil Brunner (Switzerland)." Ph.D. diss., Drew University, 1948.
146. Petri, Heinrich. "Bedeutung und Grenzen anthropologisch-personalistischer Ansaetze in der neueren Theologie." In *Wege theologischen Denkens*, ed. J. Pfammatter and F. Furger, 105–134. Zurich: Einsiedeln Benziger Verlag, 1979.
147. Pitcher, William A. "Theological Ethics in Paul Tillich and Emil Brunner: A study of the Nature of Protestant Theological Ethics." Ph.D. diss., University of Chicago, 1955.
148. Ramm, Bernard. *Types of Apologetic Systems: An Introductory Study to the Christian Philosophy of Religion*. Wheaton, Ill.: Van Kampen Press, 1953. Devotes a chapter to Brunner's apologetic methodology, classifying his work along with that of Pascal and Kierkegaard as a system "stressing subjective immediacy." A useful introduction, though it describes Brunner in terms which are inaccurate and which he would have denied, calling him "a disciple of the Barthian theology."
149. Ramsdell, E. T. Review of *The Christian Doctrine of God; Dogmatics, Vol. 1*, by Emil Brunner. In *Interpretation* 4 (October, 1950): 488–491.
150. Ramsey, Paul. *Nine Modern Moralists*. Englewood Cliffs, N.J.: Prentice Hall, 1962. Includes a chapter on Tillich and Brunner considered together.
151. Ratschhow, Carl Heinz. Review of *Dogmatik. Band 3.*, by Emil Brunner. In *Theologische Literaturzeitung* 88 (January, 1963): 1–10.
152. Reece, Robert Denton. "Religion and Morality in the

Thought of Emil Brunner." Ph.D. diss., Yale University, 1969.
153. Reif, Walter F. "The Ethical Character and Function of the Church: An Expository Dissertation of the Ethical Character and Function of the Church in the Thought of William Adams Brown, Emil Brunner, William Temple, and W. A. Visser't Hooft." Ph.D. diss., Union Theological Seminary, New York, 1954.
154. Reymond, Robert L. *Brunner's Dialectical Encounter.* An International Library of Philosophy and Theology: Biblical and Theological Studies. Philadelphia: Presbyterian and Reformed Publishing Co., 1967.
155. Ridell, John G. "Books on the Person of Christ, pt. 10; Emil Brunner, *The Mediator.*" *Expository Times* 64 (July, 1953): 292–295.
156. Robinson, Jay Patrick. "Personal Eschatology: An Analysis of Contemporary Christian Interpretations (Brunner, Boros, Cullmann, Hick, Ferre)." Ph.D. diss., Southern Baptist Theological Seminary, 1990.
157. Robinson, Laura Jo. "The role of forgiving in emotional healing: A theological and psychological analysis." Ph.D. diss. Fuller Theological Seminary, 1988. Includes reference to Brunner's understanding of forgiveness.
158. Robinson, Norman Hamilton Galloway. "Die unaufloeslichkeit der Ehe." *Zeitschrift für Evangelische Ethik* 19 (March, 1975): 102–126.
159. ———. *Faith and Duty.* New York: Harper, 1950.
160. ———. *The Groundwork of Christian Ethics.* London: Collins, 1971.
161. Roessler, Roman. *Person und Glaube: Der Personalismus der Gottesbeziehung bei Emil Brunner.* Forschungen zur Geschichte und Lehre des Protestantismus Series, ed. Ernst Wolf, no. 30. Munich: Chr. Kaiser Verlag, 1965.
162. Rolston, Holmes. *A Conservative Looks to Barth and Brunner.* Nashville: Cokesbury Press, 1933.
163. Ruhlen, Ralph Lester. "The Relationship of the Economic Order to the Moral Ideal in the Thought of Maritain, Brunner, Dewey, and Temple." Ph.D. diss., Boston University, 1959.
164. Runia, K. Review of *Dogmatics. Vol. 3: Christian Doctrine of the Church, Faith and the Consummation,* by Emil Brunner. In *Reformed Theological Review* 22 (June, 1963): 55–57.

165. Sackmann, Jacob. "Christian Redemption in the Theology of Nels Frederick Solomon Ferre: Compared with Aulen, Brunner and Dewolf." Ph.D. diss., Boston University, 1958.
166. Schneider, Erwin Eugen. "Das Mysterium der Gerechtigkeit: anlaesslich der Kritik Hans Kelsens gegen Emil Brunner." *Theologische Zeitschrift* 13 (March–April, 1957): 109–135.
167. Schmidt, Martin A. "Der Ort der Trinitaetslehre bei Emil Brunner." *Theologische Zeitschrift* 5 (January–February, 1949): 46–66.
168. Schrotenboer, Paul G. "Emil Brunner." In *Creative Minds in Contemporary Theology*, ed. Philip Edgecumbe Hughes, 99–130. Grand Rapids: Wm. B. Eerdmans Publishing Co., 1966.
169. ———. *New Apologetics: An Analysis and Appraisal of the Eristic Theology of Emil Brunner.* Kampen, Netherlands: J. H. Kok, 1955.
170. Schuurman, Douglas James. *Creation, Eschaton, and Ethics.* New York: Peter Lang Publishers Inc., 1991.
171. ———. "Creation, Eschaton and Ethics: The Ethical Significance of the Creation-Eschaton Relation in the Thought of Emil Brunner and Jurgen Moltmann." Ph.D. diss., University of Chicago, 1988.
172. Shrout, Thomas R. Review of *Letter to the Romans: A Commentary*, by Emil Brunner. In *Encounter* 22 (Winter, 1961): 100.
173. Sianipar, Frans Hanaehan. "Guilt and Its Cure: The Psychological Approaches of Sigmund Freud and Hobart Mowrer and the Theological Approach of Emil Brunner, Critically Compared." Th.D. diss., Boston University, 1964.
174. Smith, Joseph J. "Emil Brunner's Theology of Revelation." *Heythrop Journal* 6 (January, 1965): 5–26.
175. ———. *Emil Brunner's Theology of Revelation.* Manila: Loyola House of Studies, Ateneo Manila University, 1967.
176. Stampfer, Joshua. "*The Scandal of Christianity*: Reconsidered Response to Book by Emil Brunner." *Expository Times* 63 (April, 1952): 209–11.
177. Stumpf, Samuel E. "Emil Brunner's Doctrine of Law: A Study in the Theology of Law." Ph.D. diss., University of Chicago, 1949.
178. Stockwell, Clinton E. "The Ecclesiology of Emil Brunner."

Th.D. diss., New Orleans Baptist Theological Seminary, 1980.
179. Tavard, George H. "Scripture, Tradition and History." *Downside Review* 72 (no. 229, 1954): 232–44.
180. Thompson, Robert O'Hair. "The Function and Limits of Faith and Reason: A Critique of Emil Brunner's Methodology." Ph.D. diss., University of Chicago, 1970.
181. Tillich, Paul. "Questions on Brunner's epistemology." *Christian Century* 79 (October 24, 1962): 79–91. This is a reprint from *The Theology of Emil Brunner* edited by Charles W. Kegley.
182. Trittenbach, David L. "Reason and Revelation: A Discussion on their Relationship in Christian Thinking in the Light of the Writings of Tillich and of Brunner." Th.M. thesis, San Francisco Theological Seminary, 1964.
183. Tseo, Ping-I., "The Christology of Emil Brunner." Ph.D. diss., Yale University, 1941.
184. Van Til, Cornelius. *The New Modernism: An Appraisal of the Theology of Barth and Brunner*. Philadelphia: Presbyterian and Reformed Publishers, 1946. An early and critical appraisal of neo-orthodoxy from the perspective of very conservative Calvinism.
185. ———. *New Modernism: An Appraisal of the Theology of Barth and Brunner*. 2d ed. Philadelphia: Presbyterian and Reformed Publishers, 1947.
186. Vidler, Alexander Roper. Review of *The Christian doctrine of the Church, Faith and the Consummation*, by Emil Brunner. In *Theology* 66 (February, 1963): 45–46.
187. Vogelsanger, Peter, ed. *Der Auftrag der Kirche in der modernen Welt: Festgabe zum siebzigsten Geburtstag von Emil Brunner*. Zurich: Zwingli-Verlag, 1959.
188. ———. *Dank an Emil Brunner*. Zurich: Zwingli-Verlag, 1966. This volume contains a sermon by Brunner on 2 Corinthians 3.17–18.
189. Volken, Lorenz. *Der Glaube bei Emil Brunner*. Freiburg, Switzerland: Paulusverlag, 1947.
190. Ware, Bruce A. "An Evangelical Reexamination of the Doctrine of the Immutability of God." Ph.D. diss., Fuller Theological Seminary, 1984. Devotes part of the second section to examining the position of Brunner on divine immutability.
191. Westermann, Claus. "Karl Barths Nein: eine Kontroverse um

die theologia naturalis, Emil Brunner-Karl Barth (1934)." *Evangelische Theologie* 47 (September–October, 1987): 386–95.
192. Wick, Julian Dennick. "The Use of the Encounter Concept of Emil Brunner in the Curricular Thought of Christian Education." Ed.D. diss., Columbia University, 1966.
193. Wildberger, Hans. "Emil Brunner: Sein Leben und Sein Werk." *Reformatio* 31 (April, 1982): 204–17.
194. Williams, John Rodman, Jr. "The Doctrine of the 'Imago Dei' in Contemporary Theology: A Study in Karl Barth, Emil Brunner, Reinhold Niebuhr, and Paul Tillich." Ph.D. diss., Columbia University, 1954.
195. Williams, Samuel W. "Social Thought of Emil Brunner." *Journal of Religious Thought* 10 (no. 1, 1952–1953): 34–43.
196. Wing, Edward W. "Recent Tendencies in the Interpretation of the Atonement with Special Reference to Robert S. Franks, Emil Brunner, and Gustaf Aulen." Ph.D. diss., Union Theological Seminary, New York, 1953.
197. Wolf, W. J. Review of *The Christian Doctrine of God; Dogmatics, Vol. 1*, by Emil Brunner. *Anglican Theological Review* 33 (April 1951): 114–115.
198. Zimmerman, Roger William. "The Concept of Hope in Ernst Bloch and Emil Brunner." Th.D. Diss., Boston University, 1970.

SUBJECT INDEX FOR WORKS WRITTEN BY BRUNNER

Abraham, 3
alcoholism, 10, 543
angst, 13, 570, 577
anthropology, 12, 29, 83, 85, 86, 159, 160, 167, 212, 225, 226, 227, 228, 229, 230, 231, 232, 261, 262, 268, 269, 271, 276, 308, 379, 380, 381, 382, 383, 384, 403, 404, 405, 406, 407, 408, 436, 437, 438, 439, 440, 443, 444, 445, 446, 607, 641, 693
apologetics/philosophy of religion, 15, 73, 74, 75, 76, 77, 78, 79, 80, 81, 83, 156, 242, 253, 298, 299, 313, 314, 315, 426, 446, 458, 459, 460, 461, 462, 463, 464, 465, 466, 467, 477, 478, 479, 480, 504, 505, 506, 526, 527, 528, 529, 589, 590, 591, 592, 593, 594, 595, 610, 611, 620, 630, 646, 651, 652, 653, 654, 655, 656, 659, 660, 674, 675, 696
art. *See* music and art
Asia, 309, 502
autobiographical, 28, 164, 311, 549, 640

Barth, Karl, 344, 436, 437, 438, 439, 440, 443, 444, 445, 643, 644, 682, 683, 695
Bible, interpretation of, 23, 517, 518, 519, 520, 521, 545, 546, 547, 553, 626, 634, 663, 664; nature of, 46, 206, 310; Old Testament, 35, 537, 553, 584, 585, 690, 691. *See also* Romans, Book of
Blumhardt, Christoph, 108

Calvin, John, 409, 600
capitalism, 121, 122, 342, 343, 364, 365, 377, 671. *See also* economics, vocation
China, 220
Christmas, 41
church, 8, 64, 65, 66, 67, 84, 92, 97, 118, 119, 120, 148, 149, 157, 158, 162, 178, 179, 189, 211, 243, 307, 316, 342, 343, 346, 347, 348, 349, 350, 351, 352, 353, 360, 361, 362, 370, 399, 412, 413, 414, 415, 416, 433, 452, 490, 495, 509, 511, 525, 540, 541, 558, 559, 560, 586, 603, 624, 627
Church/State relations, 88, 102, 104, 105, 106, 109, 114, 115, 219, 255, 287, 357, 358, 359, 366, 499, 552, 645, 679, 686
civilization/culture/society, 55, 73, 74, 75, 76, 77, 78, 79, 80, 81, 82, 83, 84, 107, 120, 125, 127, 244, 245, 246, 247, 334, 335, 336, 337, 338, 353, 454, 672, 673
Communion, 34, 50
Communism, 14, 48, 121, 122, 190, 313, 314, 315, 363, 364, 365, 580, 581, 582, 583, 638, 639, 671

Creation, 56, 57, 58, 59, 100, 101, 144, 145, 146, 151, 190, 191, 207, 531, 532

death, 568, 569, 570
democracy, 72, 84, 240, 454, 534

economics, 22, 152, 199, 244, 245, 246, 247, 279, 280, 281, 282, 497, 531, 532, 539, 649, 678
ecumenicity/ecumenical movement, 153, 399, 498, 676, 684, 689
education, 52, 53, 71, 193, 255, 257, 283, 284, 296, 494, 650, 679
eschatology/eternal life, 97, 148, 149, 154, 186, 187, 188, 200, 201, 202, 312, 604, 605, 606, 629
ethics, 24, 136, 137, 138, 139, 140, 141, 142, 143, 189, 190, 191, 192, 193, 194, 195, 196, 199, 252, 253, 254, 256, 285, 328, 329, 352, 353, 354, 455, 548, 568, 569, 570
Europe, 198, 234, 235, 662
Eucharist. *See* Communion
evangelism, 157, 170, 180
Existentalism, 93, 94, 96, 103, 128, 159, 286, 471. *See also* Kierkegaard, Soren

faith, 64, 65, 66, 67, 95, 97, 131, 132, 133, 134, 135, 148, 149, 173, 174, 175, 176, 177, 192, 203, 204, 205, 255, 256, 257, 498, 503, 512, 513, 514, 515, 516, 650, 678
family, 207, 208, 236, 237, 258
freedom, and responsibility, 217, 218, 325, 334, 335, 336, 337, 338, 366, 403, 404, 492, 493, 534, 598

Germany, 130, 248, 362
God, 1, 60, 61, 62, 63, 69, 70, 98, 99, 144, 145, 147, 150, 190, 191, 259, 260, 264, 290, 427, 566
grace, and nature/revelation and history, 213, 249, 252, 308, 380, 381, 382, 383, 384, 403, 406, 407, 408, 436, 437, 438, 439, 440, 447, 448, 449, 512, 513, 514, 515, 516, 526, 527, 528, 529, 530, 628, 683, 688. *See also* revelation, and reason

history, views of, 239
Holy Spirit, 241, 371, 372, 373, 636, 637
hope, 110, 203, 204, 205
Huber, Max, 386

India, 263

Japan, 71, 82, 83, 84, 92, 297, 319, 320, 321, 322, 323, 324, 410, 425, 567, 586, 623, 640, 657
Jesus Christ, general works, 37, 89, 90, 110, 116, 318, 426, 387, 388, 389, 390, 391, 392, 393, 394, 395, 396, 397, 398, 418, 419, 420, 421, 422, 423, 523, 524, 620, 680; person of, 56, 57, 58, 59, 100, 101, 145, 146, 151, 387, 388, 389, 390, 391, 392, 393, 394, 395, 396, 397, 398, 418, 419, 420, 421, 422, 423, 661; resurrection, 156, 456, 457, 526, 527, 528, 529, 610, 611; uniqueness, position of 2, 4, 5, 6, 7, 387, 388, 389, 390, 391, 392, 393, 394, 395, 396, 397, 398, 418, 419, 420, 421, 422, 423; work of, 56, 57, 58, 59, 100, 101, 111, 145, 146, 151, 194, 387, 388, 389, 390, 391, 392, 393, 394, 395, 396, 397, 398, 418, 419, 420, 421, 422, 423, 526, 527, 528, 529, 666. *See also*

theology; general works; redemption
Jews/Judaism, 331, 332
justice, 244, 245, 246, 247, 334, 335, 336, 337, 338, 670

Kant, Immanuel, 286, 341
Kierkegaard, Soren, 38, 49, 286

love, 83, 165, 183, 184, 185, 203, 204, 205, 376,
Luther, Martin, 385

MacKay, John, 571
marriage, 165, 376, 555, 658
media, 251, 355, 356
miscellaneous works, 27, 36, 40, 43, 51, 54, 126, 155, 161, 168, 169, 171, 172, 181, 182, 197, 209, 210, 214, 215, 216, 238, 267, 273, 274, 278, 290, 294, 330, 339, 367, 368, 411, 417, 424, 428, 429, 434, 435, 442, 450, 453, 456, 457, 472, 473, 474, 491, 508, 510, 522, 531, 536, 538, 542, 550, 587, 588, 596, 597, 599, 601, 602, 608, 631, 635, 647, 667, 668, 677, 681, 685, 694
missions and missionaries, 32, 180, 300, 326, 540, 541, 584, 585, 687
music, and art, 31, 327, 609

Nazism, 130, 441
Niebuhr, Richard, 544
Nihilism, 11

Oxford Group, 1, 9, 16, 117, 400, 401, 402, 628

Paul, 18, 19, 20, 21
peace. *See* peace, and war
peace, and war, 221, 222, 223, 224, 341, 352, 433, 468, 469, 470, 619, 622, 642
philosophy, 475, 476

philosophy of religion. *See* apologetics, philosophy of religion]
politics, 481, 482, 499, 507, 576
prayer. *See* spiritual disciplines
Protestantism, 39, 95, 153, 369, 488, 494, 498, 500, 501, 676, 689, 692. *See also* Reformation
psychology, 47, 124, 488

race relations, 42
redemption, 56, 57, 58, 59, 100, 101, 145, 146, 151, 195. *See also* Jesus Christ, work of
Reformation. 95, 208, 345, 385, 403, 404, 495, 496, 497, 499, 500, 501, 618. *See also* Protestantism
repentance, penance, 44, 45
revelation, reason, 475, 476, 512, 513, 514, 515, 516, 526, 527, 528, 529, 696. *See also* grace, and nature/revelation and history
Roman Catholicism, 153, 498, 676, 689
Romans, Book of, 374, 375, 517, 518, 519, 520, 521, 695

Schrenk, G., 487
secularism, 525, 535
Socialism, 507
Soteriology, 196, 269, 270, 272, 318, 418, 419, 420, 421, 422, 423. *See also* redemption
spiritual disciplines, 30, 295, 692
Switzerland, 198, 234, 235, 333, 340, 450, 507, 534
symbolism, 166, 554

technology, 379, 405, 531, 532, 556
theology, general works, 12, 32, 33, 56, 57, 58, 59, 60, 61, 62, 63, 64, 65, 67, 83, 97, 98, 99, 100, 101, 145, 146, 147, 148, 149, 150, 151, 163, 173, 174, 175, 176, 177, 203, 204, 205, 213, 217,

218, 242, 248, 249, 250, 252, 258, 259, 260, 265, 266, 288, 290, 301 302, 303, 304, 305, 306, 458, 459, 460, 461 462, 463, 464, 465, 466, 467, 512, 513, 514, 515, 516, 526, 527, 528, 529, 530, 557, 561, 562, 563, 564, 565, 566, 578, 589, 590, 591, 592, 593, 594, 595, 651, 652, 653, 654, 655, 656, 665; historical, 123; liberal, 166, 277, 317, 344, 387, 388, 389, 390, 391, 392, 393, 394, 395, 396, 397, 398, 418, 419, 420, 421, 422, 423, 430, 431, 432, 554; natural. *See* grace, and nature/revelation and history; practical, 233, 258, 275, 289, 669

time, 87
truth, nature of, 131, 132, 133, 134, 135, 173, 174, 175, 176, 177, 572, 573, 574, 575, 612, 613, 614, 615, 616, 617

United States, 17, 26, 129, 198, 234, 235, 494, 579, 625

vocation, 22, 377, 539

war. *See* peace, and war
women, 378
world, place of Christian in, 25
world religions, 112, 113

youth, 68, 91, 333

ABOUT THE AUTHOR

The Reverend Doctor Mark G. McKim was born and grew up in the port city of Saint John, New Brunswick on Canada's east coast. Since 1990 he has served as the minister of the historic Germain Street United Baptist Church in Saint John. He is actively involved in ecumenical and community activities, serving, for example as President of the Downtown Ministers' Association. He also has a strong interest in theological education, and is a member of both the Board of Trustees, and Senate, of his alma mater, Acadia Divinity College.

Dr. McKim holds the degrees of Bachelor of Arts, in history and political science, with distinction, from the University of New Brunswick, Master of Divinity, with honors, from Acadia Divinity College, Acadia University, and Doctor of Theology from Boston University. He has published articles in a number of scholarly and popular level journals.